ADVANCE PRAISE

"Like its great title, Don't Leave a Mess! has one outstanding element often missing in books about financial advice: its clear readability. Sandy Pollack writes in a straightforward, commonsense voice, easily conveying complex issues and recommendations in a very natural style. She boils things down to their essence without oversimplifying, using stories and examples to help explain things. If you want to read one book on family legacy planning, make it Don't Leave a Mess!"

—James Grubman, PhD, family wealth consultant and author of *Strangers in Paradise: How Families Navigate Wealth Across Generations*

"This book is a wonderful resource for entrepreneurs and family business leaders. Sandy shares real-life stories which illustrate how easily things can go wrong, and then she follows up with clear, actionable advice to help us avoid disaster. Sandy also invites us to be courageous and to have regular, open conversations with our families so that we can 'Leave a Legacy' instead of 'Leaving a Mess!'"

—David C. Bentall, President of Nextstep Advisors and FFI (Family Firm Institute) fellow

"It's rare that a book delivers on its title. Don't Leave a Mess! not only delivers a powerful message about why we should organize our affairs, but it also tells us how. If implementing the ideas in this book weren't so simple, the devastation to family wealth from procrastination wouldn't be so sad. A must-read."

—Tom Deans, PhD, author of *Willing Wisdom* and *Every Family's Business*

"Most family business owners, particularly founders (Gen 1), avoid putting plans in place to deal with transition and succession. For various reasons, they struggle with knowing where to start and how to engage and communicate with their family to make rational decisions that will protect their legacy and wealth. The unfortunate outcome is a real mess for their family to clean up after they are gone. In this book, Don't Leave a Mess!, Sandy draws on her tremendous experience advising families to provide real-life strategies and guidance on how to successfully navigate planning your legacy. Her compelling stories and direct, no-nonsense approach will help family business owners overcome their procrastination and inertia to develop a true legacy-thinking mindset."

—Bill Brushett, President and CEO of Family Enterprise Canada

"Silence is easy; opening up is hard. NOW GET MOVING! Written with a disarming combination of empathy and tough-mindedness, this book is a soup-to-nuts guidebook for the business-owning family. Need some ideas on how to start talking about money in your family? On picking the right advisors and getting rid of the wrong ones? On managing your own emotions while you do these tasks? The author provides grounded, practical strategies on everything it takes to do the hard, right things."

—Moira Somers, PhD, C.Psych, author of *Advice That Sticks*

"This book provides insight into the passion and commitment Sandra has towards family and business. Sandra guides you through some tried and true steps that have served her clients well and provided them with a path towards successful continuity in business, wealth, and most importantly, family cohesion."

—Susan St Amand, TEP, FEA, ICD.D, Board Chair of Family Enterprise Canada, Executive in Residence at Telfer School of Management at University of Ottawa Family Enterprise Legacy Institute, and President of Sirius Group Inc.

DON'T LEAVE A MESS!

DON'T LEAVE A MESS!

How to Disaster-Proof Your Family Legacy

SANDY POLLACK
CFP, CLU, TEP, FEA, MFA-P

LIONCREST
PUBLISHING

COPYRIGHT © 2022 SANDY POLLACK
All rights reserved.

DON'T LEAVE A MESS!

How to Disaster-Proof Your Family Legacy

ISBN	978-1-5445-3666-8	*Hardcover*
	978-1-5445-3667-5	*Paperback*
	978-1-5445-3668-2	*Ebook*

To my husband and partner for life,
my everything, Steven Poleski.
I am thankful for the legacy we created together.
Thank you for putting up with me.

To Talia, Adam, and Danielle,
my petri dish for meaningful (and awkward)
conversations. I love you all.

CONTENTS

INTRODUCTION 1

CHAPTER ONE
THE PRICE OF SILENCE
When families can't talk about money, it hurts everyone. 11

CHAPTER TWO
UNDERSTAND YOUR STORY AND SHARE IT
Your history shapes your wealth building journey. Your family needs to understand that journey, and what wealth means to you. 31

CHAPTER THREE
GIVING WITH PURPOSE
Plan your wealth to include the causes that matter to you. 51

CHAPTER FOUR
A LEGACY OF STEWARDSHIP
Your complex family enterprise is a responsibility. Prepare your family to understand and become stewards of wealth. 71

CHAPTER FIVE
PICK YOUR ADVISORY TEAM
Your professional advisors need to collaborate, not just cooperate. 105

CHAPTER SIX
TAXES: TRUTH OR CONSEQUENCES
Financial freedom and estate planning are about more than avoiding taxes. 137

CHAPTER SEVEN
CONSIDER HUMAN CAPITAL RISK
Bad things happen in life, so you need to be prepared. 155

CHAPTER EIGHT
GET IT IN WRITING
Your legacy planning includes legal documents and personal instructions to make sure your family isn't left in the dark. 181

CHAPTER NINE
YOU'RE NEVER DONE TILL YOU'RE IN THE BOX
Review your plans regularly so you can stay current and relevant in the changes of life. 209

CONCLUSION 223

ACKNOWLEGMENTS 229

ABOUT THE AUTHOR 233

INTRODUCTION

The air in the room buzzed with tension. As they sat waiting for the lawyer to join them, the family stole glances at each other, but nobody spoke. The widow, exhausted as she was, perched awkwardly in her chair. The past weeks had been a nightmare.

She looked over at her eldest son sitting beside her. He patted her arm, but it wasn't much comfort. He'd been working in his father's business for ten years, but he didn't know any more about the finances than she did.

Those miserable days between the hospital and the funeral, when all she wanted to do was spend time with her grandchildren, had been taken up instead with searching for paperwork: the will, the life insurance policies—she wasn't even sure where the business checkbook was, or how the employees got paid on time. They'd torn apart both the home office and the business office. They searched every desk drawer, cupboard, and filing cabinet. Eventually they'd found the safe-deposit key. Thank goodness she was authorized to use it, or they would never have found the will at all.

And in the end, it wasn't even the correct version of the will! She'd been so worried and upset, she couldn't remember when they last updated their estate plans. At least the old copy gave them the name and address of the attorney. He'd retired, but a new partner took over their file. Now here they sat in a cold conference room, waiting for this stranger to explain how their lives were going to change.

Finally, the lawyer bustled in with a fat file of papers and started in on a long, dry recitation of legal gibberish. The widow tried to pay attention, but the whole thing didn't make much sense. She knew her husband owned a business, but now it sounded like there were several different companies. She recognized some of the names, and others she didn't. She knew they had some rental real estate because she recalled signing papers, but now it sounded like she didn't even really own it. And what about their home? And the family cottage?

Before she could ask any questions, the lawyer was talking about financial bequests. Everyone gasped when he named the sums. She knew they were comfortable, but this? They were rich! He was talking about tens of millions of dollars.

She looked around. Her children were dumbfounded. And then, as the list of bequests to individuals and organizations went on, the shock turned to confusion.

"Wait a minute!" her middle son blurted out. "Who are these people? Are these charities? Why are they even getting a share?"

His sister, the youngest of the three, snapped at him, "Don't be greedy."

"Well, have you ever heard of them?" he snapped back.

She shrugged. Not a clue.

The attorney looked over his glasses. "Well, this document was drawn up fifteen years ago."

The eldest was out of his chair now, pacing. "I don't believe it. I've been busting my ass at that company for half of what I could make anywhere else, just to keep the place afloat. And all this time, Dad's loaded!" He turned to his mother, and she could see the pain in his eyes, behind the anger. "Was he just screwing me over?"

Now all three siblings were staring at their mother. "Mom, did you know?"

She just shook her head. All she could think was that this wasn't what her husband would have wanted. Why didn't he tell her how much he had? Or what his intentions were? Why didn't they take the time to talk about this more? If only they'd had more time to talk things over.

If only they had more time.

If only we had more time. I hear this phrase much too often. In all the years I've been a financial advisor, I have yet to witness anyone die at the "right" time.

Unfortunately, stories like this are all too typical: An entrepreneur pours their heart and soul into building up a successful family business enterprise but leaves a mess behind when they're gone.

The remaining family members have no idea how to pull together the pieces of their family business legacy. Worse, they have no idea why the wealth builder made the decisions they did, or what they were thinking. They don't know what it all means. They haven't just suffered a heartbreaking loss—everything left to deal with in its wake is a disaster.

IT'S NOT TOO LATE

If you're reading this book, congratulations—you're alive! That means you still have time to get things right. Maybe you've done very well in business, but you have this nagging feeling in the back of your mind that your future plans are lacking. Or maybe you're starting out in business and are on a trajectory to success, but finding it hard to navigate the legal, tax, and personal complexity of the family enterprise you're building.

You have a successful family business enterprise, but there's only a superficial connection between your family, your business, and your wealth. You may have a comprehensive tax plan, but you don't have a plan to communicate your legacy to your loved ones. You're very busy, you don't have time to study estate planning, and you don't know where to start. You need someone to ask you the right thought-provoking questions, uncover the gaps in your planning, and help you connect the dots.

BECOMING DISASTER-PROOF

The solution is simple: get your plans in order and explain them to your family. Easier said than done, I know! There are deep cultural taboos and personal discomfort around discussing money, especially if you started life with very little of it and built your wealth with hard work, tenacity, and grit.

There can also be major disconnects between parents and their children around careers, money, gifts, or life choices. All of this comes down to a misalignment in values and communication that can cause misunderstandings and conflict. Often these conflicts get amplified by chaos, confusion, and grief after a death. That creates an even bigger disaster: families have the potential to turn on each other and be torn apart. This is why estate litigation is a growth industry in North America.

Your true legacy is found in the *values* you pass to your children, not just the valuables. They need to understand your challenges, important moments, and triumphs in order to understand the choices you made to provide for them. Your values are the DNA of your legacy planning. They are your True North. They guide (or should guide) your family wealth, your charitable giving, your business succession plans, your tax and estate plans, your choice of advisors, and how diligently you prepare for the future.

This book will teach you a mindset and a process that I call **Legacy Thinking**. I'll help you dig deep to find the real meaning behind your decisions in the past and your plans for the future. You'll learn to understand your history and communicate to your family the true story of how you built your business—and, more importantly, why.

I'll show you how sharing your story—good and bad—can instill confidence and resilience in your children. I'll help you think about how to prepare the next generation to apply their resources constructively; how to step up in your family enterprise; and how to be good stewards of the legacy you leave them. You'll discover how to build a collaborative team of professional advisors who can create financial and legal plans tailored to your vision and values. I'll help you examine your long-term financial hopes, risks, and needs, and plan for them effectively. The best-laid plans are useless if they just sit in a desk drawer, so I'll show you how to select a head coach who will make sure you execute those plans and communicate them to your loved ones.

You'll also learn practical strategies to ensure your family is on the same page and have the tools they need to secure a self-reliant future, ensure their well-being, and be good citizens.

Specifically, I'll address some of the most frequently asked questions I get from my clients:

- How do I protect what I have worked so hard during the course of my lifetime to build?
- If something happens to me, how do I ensure that my family will be taken care of? Does the plan make sense?
- Is it wise to leave my business and all of my wealth to my children?
- What's "fair"? How do I rationalize passing the business on to one child who wants to manage, while my other children are not actively working or contributing to the business?
- How can I guarantee the business will be able to carry on without me while ensuring my financial security and maintaining family harmony?
- Do my wills, corporate structure, and other legal plans reflect my values, my family's values, and address my family's overall financial security?
- If I die unexpectedly, will my business partners be able to pay my family fairly and promptly for my shares?

There are no one-size-fits-all answers to these questions, but with Legacy Thinking and the right advisors, you can find answers that are tailored to you and your situation.

LIFELONG LEARNING

The ideas and strategies I'm going to share with you are hard-won from more than thirty years working as a financial advisor for business owners and their family enterprises. These insights and advice are also intensely personal.

I grew up in a big, blended Jewish-Italian family with not much money but a whole lot of motivation. Both of my parents worked hard throughout my childhood to put food on the table and a roof over our heads. I knew I'd have to make my own way if I wanted to pursue a postsecondary education. Summers, I worked one job Monday to Friday and another on the weekends. During the school year, I worked part-time so I could keep saving for university. I learned the importance of playing the long game and making wise choices at a young age. (Sometimes those lessons were from the School of Hard Knocks.)

In university, I flirted with the idea of becoming a labor relations lawyer. Unfortunately, I discovered that I have no poker face for negotiation; I'm too much of an open book. Instead, I started in the insurance business and learned the most important skills that I still use every day: curiosity, persistence, and asking "why?" I don't consider myself exceptionally gifted, but I am a world-class noodge. I finish what I start, and I make sure my clients get their planning finished, too—on their own terms, not mine.

When I started my solo practice, I'd just moved from Montreal to Ottawa and knew nobody. When my husband and I purchased our first home and decided to renovate, I started talking with the contractors. Every time I had a conversation, I'd listen to their stories, their problems, and their worries, so I could understand how to help them. I'd also ask them to introduce me to their lawyer, their accountant, and other business owners. As my practice grew, I threw myself into continuing education and became qualified as a Certified Financial Planner, a Chartered Life Underwriter, a Trust and Estate Practitioner, and a Family Enterprise Advisor. I hold a master's in Financial Advising for Philanthropy, and I'm a member of the Purposeful Planning Institute, as well as many other professional organizations.

I didn't know what the hell I was doing when I first started, but this industry is one where people open their hearts if their advisor cares enough to ask the right questions. Often, clients tell me the things that are keeping them awake at night. A good advisor has to open their ears—and their heart—to listen and build trust.

It's amazing the number of professional advisors who forget to ask deep questions, and just want to get the job done. My passion is to help people. Getting to know and understand my clients long-term is the best part of my work. A true financial advisor is involved to some degree in every major aspect of someone's life: business planning, partnerships, estate planning, new home purchases, as well as family changes like marriage and children. We're involved in the difficult times, too: divorce, business breakups or losses, illness, and death. That cradle-to-grave perspective has enabled me to stay grounded and realistic about the significance of planning your future well, and the urgency of putting those plans into action.

THINK DEEPLY, ACT DECISIVELY

If you're an entrepreneur, I know you work incredibly hard at building your family business enterprise. I also understand how every day is a day filled with problem solving, critical decision-making, and keeping your sanity amidst chaos. I'm not going to waste your time with a bunch of touchy-feely fluff. This book isn't generic, cookie-cutter advice to read, nod over, and then leave on the shelf to collect dust.

I want to light a fire under you. Whether you're worth a million or a hundred million, I want you to stop and think—to reflect on what you've built, how you got to this point in your life, and how you can create an intentional, meaningful legacy. Then I want you to get up off your butt and make it happen. Life is messy, and it's inevitable that there will be some loose ends and gaps in anyone's long-term plans. You get to choose whether that gap is a buttonhole or a gaping quarry—an inconvenience, or a disaster.

After all, the most important part of your family's legacy isn't their financial inheritance. It's the values that you've taught them, ensuring family harmony and shared purpose. The success of your planning depends on your choice to engage in healthy conversations, so you can communicate your intentions, values, and, most of all, your love for them.

I want to challenge your thinking. If I can get you to think differently about one aspect of your legacy planning, and then get you to take one step forward and put those plans into action, I'll count that as a win. None of us are guaranteed tomorrow. Today you still have a chance to connect with your family, communicate your vision, and avert disastrous family conflicts and ugly, costly messes.

If you have questions or concerns about a particular aspect of your planning, feel free to skip directly to that chapter and dive into the topic that's most relevant to your situation right now. Anything that will get you moving, go for it! But I hope you will go back and read all of the chapters, because there are important details in each one, and they all work together to take you on a journey.

The first step of that journey begins now.

WISE WORDS

"The truth hurts, but silence kills."

—*Mark Twain*

CHAPTER ONE

THE PRICE OF SILENCE

When families can't talk about money, it hurts everyone.

Teddy Libfeld was a textbook example of a self-made success story. A survivor of Auschwitz, he immigrated to Canada in the 1950s and built a construction business into a real-estate development empire. His company, the Conservatory Group, grew to more than 350 holding companies and joint ventures that included residential and commercial real estate, as well as mortgage lending. In 2021, the total enterprise was valued between $2.5 and $4 billion. Clearly, Mr. Libfeld was incredibly good at building and managing his business.

Although he was often described as a loving father and charming, thoughtful entrepreneur, he did not do so well at instilling healthy, independent relationships among his children. He seems to have been the mortar that kept the family together. When Mr. Libfeld died in 2000, he left his four sons as equal owners of the enterprise, without any defined roles or plans for succession, governance, or dispute resolution mechanisms.

The power struggles between the children began almost immediately. By 2005 they brought in teams of professional advisors to try to put some written agreements in place to govern their working relationships. It didn't help.

Their disagreements over how to run the business led to bitter personal disputes and a complete breakdown of family relations, up to and including fistfights in the company boardroom. For the last four years of its life, the enterprise was unable to enter into any new transactions due to this stalemate among the owners. It also failed to pay the correct amount of taxes. The legal battles raged for years, until the court finally ordered the whole enterprise to be liquidated because there was no way for the brothers to operate the business constructively.

Instead of a multi-billion-dollar legacy that could secure his family's future for generations, Mr. Libfeld's lifetime of hard work dissolved in acrimony, legal fees, and hundreds of millions in back taxes and interest penalties. No cash settlement from the liquidation of this business could ever replace the blood, sweat, and tears that went into building it, or the incredible opportunities that were wasted.

One of the most contentious points raised by the judge in the final order of Libfeld vs. Libfeld was a dispute over the founder's intentions for his legacy. Two of the brothers asserted that their father would have wanted the business to continue as a single group, even if all the brothers didn't participate. The other two said that he would have wanted all the brothers to participate, even if the business were divided into separate enterprises. They couldn't even agree on how to divide the business holdings, all because they each had a different understanding of their father's legacy.

Reading the media coverage of this spectacular family enterprise implosion, it's very sad. It's quite obvious that the brothers loved and revered their father enormously. However, each had different interpretations of what their father wanted, because—for whatever reason—it seems as though they didn't have this important conversation while he was alive.

The Libfeld family's enormous success—and their heart-wrenching, public disintegration—have been talking points in the financial news for the last decade. The media coverage might give the impression that this business and relational meltdown is rare and newsworthy. After thirty years as a financial advisor, I assure you that while this story is sensational because of its massive scale, it is by no means rare.

> **Silence is the root cause of every mess
> I see in a family enterprise.**

When families can't talk about money, it hurts everyone. I've reached a juncture in my business where I've seen so many broken, divided families, so much anger and resentment, and so many preventable disasters, that I'm fed up. I'm tired of seeing the carnage, and I want to do everything in my power to break that cycle. If this book saves one family—your family—from a similar fate, I'll be happy.

Contingency planning, family business transition, business succession, family legacy and estate planning, are all pretty big words. These big words cannot change the fact that what we're really talking about is our own mortality, which is a deeply emotional and distressing topic. Nobody wants to talk about it. Nobody enjoys talking about it. We put it off, we avoid the subject, we focus on the present moment and try not to think about the future. Ever have a dinner conversation and say, "Let's talk about death"? Not likely.

Let's call it what it is: **death**. The topic is too important to mince words.

Nobody rushes to the cemetery to buy a plot. When we have a toothache, on the other hand, we rush to the dentist because we feel the pain. Your silence about your wealth and your plans isn't a pain you feel right now. It's a time bomb, ticking away, that could blow your family apart. I'm here to make sure you hear the ticking, feel the discomfort, and do something about it.

Silence is the root cause of every mess I see in a family enterprise. In every case, the founder, though incredibly courageous and successful in building their business, failed to adequately educate their family about money, or prepare them by communicating their values, vision, and plans for the future. The only way to disaster-proof your legacy is to break that silence.

There are many reasons why it's hard to talk about your wealth with your family. Frankly, silence is easy, while meaningful, intentional communication is hard. A plethora of unspoken myths and cultural taboos make talking about wealth (and talking about death) intensely uncomfortable. Nevertheless, you must—you absolutely *must*—find a way to overcome those obstacles. Your silence may be comfortable, it may be a matter of habit, but in the long run your silence will come at a devastating cost.

Throughout this chapter, I'm going to pose a lot of questions to help you uncover how the various reasons for silence may be invisibly at work in your own life. I encourage you to stop and think about your responses, jot down your answers, and make special note of the points that hit home. I want you to participate with me in this process. I want you to take action. Think, reflect, and do.

SILENCE IS EASY

There's a trap some of my clients fall into when thinking about their estate and business succession planning. They understand that they *should* have these important conversations with their family. They agree that these plans and documents *need* to get done. They listen, they nod, they smile.

Nothing happens.

Remember, these are entrepreneurs! They're action-takers, problem-solvers extraordinaire, with resilience and tenacity that could be bottled and sold. Their fortunes are built on their ability to execute, to *get shit done*. Somehow, though, they can't seem to wedge enough time into their busy schedules to get their will and estate plans completed. They keep saying they'll get it done later, and later often comes too late.

I have a client who's worth about $25 million, and he hates it when I draw up his net worth statement. He can't stand to look at it, because he says, "That's not me!"

He drives an old car. He has a $2 million home and a $1 million vacation property in Arizona, but he's still driving a ten-year-old Volvo. That net worth statement may not reflect *who he is*, but it is the reality of *what he has built*, and what he owns. He has to deal with it. Avoiding reality might seem like a way to make your life simpler, but it doesn't make the value disappear. The same is true of your legacy planning. Taking the easy road now is just avoiding reality; it doesn't erase your responsibility.

Entrepreneurs spend so much time solving day-to-day problems in their business and growing its value that they want easy solutions for everything else. A tax problem? Call the accountant. A legal problem? Call the lawyer. But planning a complex family enterprise is so much bigger than one phone call to one professional. Honestly, most people would rather just ignore it.

I get it. It's so much easier to go back to the office and focus on building another plant, buying another building, selling another widget, or starting another business! That's the default. It's also more fun—who doesn't get a charge out of creating something bigger than what you already have, particularly if you started from nothing? But if you don't even consider making incremental changes to thinking about the bigger picture, you'll leave a disaster behind.

> **With success comes responsibility—to your family, to your employees, and to your community.**

The easiest thing in the world is to write a simple, boilerplate will that leaves everything to your spouse—boom, done. Let the next generation sort it out. The thing is, that's only easy for the person who dies first. The last person standing has to deal with all the crap. If you don't make the time to sit down with your spouse or your adult children and talk about the extent of your wealth, the breadth of your enterprise, your intentions, their responsibilities, and your values, you aren't doing them any favors.

Most wealth builders don't have those conversations because they don't know where to start. They're afraid of letting a stranger into their world who might judge them (or might just want to sell them a product or service, and then run off when the job is done). They feel alone and don't know who to trust.

OPENING UP IS HARD

Many entrepreneurs are uncomfortable discussing their wealth with their family because they didn't grow up having those conversations.

A background of challenges and difficulty can often light the fire that launches a person to success, but it also leaves a gap in their own experiences. In his book *Strangers in Paradise*, James Grubman talks about the differences between "natives to wealth" and "strangers to wealth." Without a natural model for how to talk about money, some wealth holders simply don't know where to begin.

Thomas J. Stanley and William D. Danko address a similar concept in their book, *The Millionaire Next Door*. They use the term PAWs—Prodigious Accumulators of Wealth. These self-made millionaires tend to live below their means and choose their luxuries carefully. As a result, their modest lifestyle is the tip of an iceberg of affluence. They've kept their finances private all along, as a defense mechanism against the dysfunctionality and grief they've seen money bring to others. This habit makes it very uncomfortable for them to acknowledge what they've built, even to themselves. Uncovering that iceberg for their family is such a challenge, they'd rather put it off and watch the Super Bowl.

That seems similar to what happened with Teddy Libfeld and his family. Based on my own experiences with entrepreneurs from Mr. Libfeld's generation, I can't help but wonder how the trauma of his experiences shaped his attitude to business and his ability to communicate with his family. There's a mindset common to this cohort that emphasizes self-reliance, but to a point that it backfires on them. They are so accustomed to fending for themselves that they pass up opportunities to open up or get help, even when it's freely available.

These survivors love their children deeply, but that stubborn independence can make them short-sighted and ultimately block them from what they're trying to do—create financial security and greater opportunities for their children. Their own experiences of loss make it hard for them to fathom how siblings could fight or split apart. They don't prepare for it because it's unimaginable for them. This happens as well with first- and second-generation business owners that have immigrated to a new country. Because they left so much behind to give their family a better life, it's unthinkable that the next generation would be unable to work together in a harmonious and respectful way.

A TWO-WAY STREET

Conversations about generational wealth are uncomfortable from both directions. In my industry, we refer to family wealth in much the same way that people talk about immigration: first generation, second generation, and so forth (or G1, G2, G3 for short). For an adult child or grandchild (the second or third generation), it can be intimidating to ask about the founder's wishes and their estate plan. They may have the best of intentions, but there's a real concern, too. "Will Dad think I'm just being greedy? Will Mom feel this is disrespectful? What if they think I'm too nosy and just want their money?"

From the wealth builder's side, you've carried so much responsibility for so many years that you're used to shouldering the burden alone. You don't feel right about placing it on your spouse or children. You understand all the worries and stresses of managing your business, the day-to-day struggles of landlords, tenants, vendors, partners, negotiation, and compromise. You want to protect your loved ones from those responsibilities—because you have always taken care of things. Perhaps your marriage has worked so well all these years because you each stayed in your lane, but it can't work like that forever. Now is the time to share that information and teach them how to manage this wealth, because you won't always be here to carry the load and protect them.

In every generation, I see discomfort that's rooted in fear—fear of unraveling who you are, where you came from, and how you became successful. Nine times out of ten, the clients I meet who have built great wealth did so from humble beginnings. They may be trying to outrun childhood poverty, or they may have left their home country to start a new life. They left their roots behind to create a bigger future for themselves and their families. Building and focusing on the future is fun. But the thing they need to stop and think about, unpack and share with their loved ones, is exactly what they're running from: their past. Their story. Their hardships, and the failures they experienced along the way. Your family needs to see the full arc of where you're coming from and where you're trying to go in order to carry on your legacy in a meaningful and responsible way.

DISPELLING MYTHS

Some of those fears take the form of unspoken beliefs or myths. Often, these myths are powerful precisely because they're never articulated or examined. When you say them out loud or read them in black and white, it's easy to see that they're false (or even a bit ridiculous).

As you read through this list, consider which of these myths might be holding you back. Maybe you are dealing with more than one, or maybe you have some other fears and superstitions that aren't mentioned. Whatever mental blocks might stand in your way, let's shine a light on them and break the spell.

MYTH #1: THE JINX

This is a feeling that most people would never express out loud, because they know it's irrational—but it's still a real roadblock, because our irrational feelings are the strongest. It's the fear that *if I write my will, I'm going to die*, or *if I buy life insurance, it means I'm going to die*.

The truth is, with 100 percent certainty, there is one life per person, and one death per person. The problem is, we don't know when that death will occur, and we don't get to choose our moment. We *do* get to choose whether we leave our families taken care of, or whether we leave them a big, honking mess. I have yet to meet a person who's died the day after signing their will or bought a life insurance policy.

The myth tells you, *if I don't prepare, it won't happen*. The reality is that it will happen anyway, plus you'll be unprepared when it does.

Trying to avoid the jinx *is* the jinx.

I understand this fear exists, but I personally believe the opposite is true: just like carrying an umbrella magically stops it from raining, I feel like writing one's will, or securing life insurance and critical illness insurance, makes people live longer and stay healthier. This may sound just as superstitious, but it moves people in the right direction and provides peace of mind.

MYTH #2: THE RIVAL

You'd be surprised how frequently this one comes up. A lot of the business owners I help are secretly afraid of being replaced after they're dead and gone. The fear is that *if I leave my wife too much money, she'll remarry and some other schmuck will get it, instead of my kids*.

If this thought worries you, you're not alone. Think of it this way: all the more reason to plan your estate properly, to make sure your children and grandchildren are provided for, instead of the money being diverted into a different family. If you don't have a plan in place, then you get no say at all over where that money winds up. Get it done properly, and you can stop worrying about the other schmuck.

If it makes you feel better, I've often had interesting conversations where a spouse says that after thirty years of marriage, they never want to walk down the aisle again.

MYTH #3: SUPERMAN

Entrepreneurs are the most resilient and positive human beings on the planet. I have seen them deal with recessions, catastrophes, pandemics, divorces, competitors, and changes in industry, and they still manage to navigate these challenging waters and end up better off than they were before the storm. Even so, we are all human and we all have our limits.

Nobody likes admitting they're vulnerable. Nobody likes imagining bad things in their future. It's scary, worrisome, and it saps our energy. Out of sight, out of mind, right? Some people seem to convince themselves *they'll never get sick*. That denial lasts right up until they get the dreaded phone call from their doctor to come in for a consultation and review their test results.

I suppose it's possible that a person might never get sick. Some people go quite suddenly, but that's the exception rather than the rule. There's a randomness to illness and mortality that we fail to understand until it touches someone within our circle. The randomness and ferocity of cancer seem to strike even young people more and more these days. This disease in particular knows no bounds of age or sex. The survival rate is getting better all the time, but the financial impact can be devastating and last for years.

Most of the things that could kill you don't kill you, at least not right away—that includes accidents, illness, and disability. You could pull through, but you'll need some kind of provision in place to take care of your family and your business while you recover, not to mention paying for your treatments and care. And when you do eventually die (whether it's of sickness or something quick and clean), you still need to have your affairs in order.

MYTH #4: MISPLACED HUMILITY

Some people avoid estate planning because they tell themselves *I'm not that important. I don't have that much. I'm replaceable.* Sometimes it's because they've never really sat down to take inventory of all the assets they've built and everything they actually do. Their mindset is stuck in a time warp dating back to the period when they were just starting out (with the addition of a nicer home, nicer vehicle, and perhaps a cottage or other toys). They're future-based, so they see themselves as still on a trajectory to success. Others believe they've done such a good job delegating responsibility at work and at home that everything can run just fine without them.

When I hear this, I ask, "If that's the case, why are you still showing up to the office at 6:00 a.m.? Why are you still working nights and weekends, and taking business calls when you're supposed to be on vacation? If you aren't important, why are you there at all? Can't the business manage itself?"

Eventually, the truth reveals itself that the successful entrepreneur is like the rebar in a concrete foundation. They really *are* that important to keep the operations running smoothly. Ironically, the people who are loath to open up and put their plans (and disaster plans) in writing are the least able to step away. They haven't really delegated authority because there's so much knowledge locked up in their own heads.

Humility is a virtue, but if you're disconnected from the truth of your situation, it will lead you astray. Taking responsibility isn't arrogant, it's the right thing to do for your business, your employees, and your family. Get your planning done with the same diligence you bring to your business, and then you can rest easy.

MYTH #5: MIND YOUR MANNERS

Some people avoid talking about their estate with their family because down deep they believe that *it's not nice to talk about money*. This false assumption that talking about money is rude is trained into us from childhood, because there's an absence of money conversations around the dinner table.

Money is an important component of everyday life. We need money to eat. We need money for shelter. We need it to play and take vacations. We need it to help others through charity or in our communities.

Your relationship with money is a fundamental part of your identity. Unknowingly, we express our priorities and values in the way we deploy money, so it behooves us to be able to articulate those values. It's never too late to teach your children financial literacy and share the values that created them. It's more than nice—it's mandatory, like breathing. Having money conversations at an early age teaches your children about patience, goals, self-discipline, choices, charity, security, freedom, and priorities. Don't put it off.

MYTH #6: SOMEDAY

The biggest myth on the list is that *someday, I will get all of this taken care of*. *Someday* is the magical time when all the things you know *should* happen, and *need* to happen, will somehow get done (possibly by invisible fairies). I hate to tell you, but the magic fairies aren't coming—they're too busy managing the magic fairy kingdom (which isn't very profitable). There is no guarantee that Someday will ever come. You only have Today. The time to get your planning done is right now.

THE PRICE IS HIGH

Leaving your family without insight or clear direction is like leaving them in the woods with nothing but a trail of breadcrumbs to find their way out. Perhaps they will find their way. Perhaps they'll stay lost or encounter a wolf that takes advantage of their situation. The price of silence is that your loved ones feel like they're drowning in confusion, on top of drowning in grief.

When the second or third generation finds out that there's an unexpected amount of money coming their way, it can knock them sideways. They aren't prepared to handle the enormity of the gift because they weren't mentored. There's often guilt and remorse attached to that inheritance, particularly if their relationship with their parents or grandparents was challenging. They may not even understand how much their parent actually loved them.

The myth of successful entrepreneurs being superheroes runs deep. Often, the kids or grandkids of a successful, driven entrepreneur struggle with feelings of inadequacy while their parents are living. Unconsciously, they use their parents' success as a measuring stick and find themselves falling short. After years of feeling like they can't measure up to expectations, they may even wash their hands of the relationship. A surprise inheritance of millions of dollars can create intense feelings of guilt: *Should I have been more patient? Should I have tried harder to make the relationship work?* So much regret could be avoided if the parent would share their dreams, their goals, their history, their struggles, and their values with their children.

Your values and resilience led you to build a thriving business and create security for your family. The values have to come before the money. Unless you share and intentionally communicate those values with your children, they may lack confidence and be without a North Star ahead of them. Without that guide, the money may lead them astray. They'll blow it. Some might snort it, some might drink or gamble it, and some might just fritter it away on foolish decisions.

It's normal to feel conflicted about your wealth and how to transfer it to your family with wisdom. Any important, complicated plan involves a lot of decisions, a lot of options to weigh, and a lot of pros and cons. Don't turn away from that conflict! It's uncomfortable, but it's the only way to move forward.

Conflict isn't fun, but sometimes it's necessary and beneficial. For example, if you have an argument with your spouse, that can be a healthy conflict. You each air your opinions. Eventually, you'll reach some kind of resolution (or not). Maybe one of you is persuaded. Maybe you get a different perspective and decide the issue wasn't that important. The important thing is that you both feel heard. It's a productive conversation. The same is true in planning your legacy—all those conflicting ideas and feelings need to be heard and talked out, so you can reach a resolution and move on.

WILL YOU TAKE THE LEAP?

Of course, nobody intends to leave a mess behind. They need help, encouragement, guidance, and perhaps even someone to facilitate those conversations.

Family harmony doesn't just happen by accident, it takes time and attention. Conflict is an inherent factor in any family, and harmony ebbs and flows. A communication breakdown is like an infection. You can't see it, but it can be in the air all around you. It can usually be cleared up if you catch it early, but once it festers, you're in trouble. You might wind up with a permanent scar or even an amputation.

> **Family harmony doesn't happen by accident.**

If you haven't already had a series of values-based conversations with your kids about your wealth, it can seem difficult to get started. Maybe you need a facilitator. Maybe you need a team of therapists—I don't know what your situation is like. These days, we recognize that mental health (including good communication and relationships) is just as important as lifting weights or getting your teeth cleaned.

It takes courage to reach outside your comfort zone and ask for help, but as the founder, it's your responsibility to do exactly that. There is good counsel and guidance available to help you navigate these complex issues. For your own good and the long-term survival of your family, take the help. You must be open to having difficult conversations. When you do, you may actually find they aren't just difficult—they're transformational.

STOP, THINK, START

Entrepreneurs are visionaries. When they have a vision, they will go over, under, around, and through to get where they want to go. And in their quest for success and wealth, they become expert problem-solvers. They deal with a plethora of problems every day: wake up, deal with a problem, and on to the next one. It's like a muscle contraction, they just get things done.

Planning for your family legacy (business or personal) isn't something you can check off your daily to-do list in one squeeze, and it's not a problem you can solve by hiring one person to handle everything for you. If running your business is like keeping a ship on course, then family business and estate legacy planning is an iceberg. You can't just maneuver around the bit you see in front of you, because that's only a fraction of the matter. You have to take time to comprehend the full magnitude of your situation.

No matter what you achieve in life, your family will remember the personal side of your legacy more than the public or material side. If you leave a mess behind, the rest of the world may remember your accomplishments or your philanthropy, but the people you love most will remember the disaster you created. You've sacrificed too much for your family to throw it all away like that. Instead, dismantle your wall of silence. It feels risky, but I promise you that risk brings a huge reward.

Take time to reflect on what you have, how much you have, and what you want to do with it. When you're ready to break your silence, you can truly engage in the process of Legacy Thinking. That starts with digging deep into your personal story so you can understand yourself. Then you can share your story—share yourself—with your family.

# HOMEWORK

Remember when I asked you to ponder the questions raised in this chapter and write down your answers? Here's a summary to make it easier. I encourage you to continue adding to those answers as you work through the following chapters.

- If you didn't wake up tomorrow morning, would your spouse and children be able to keep your business running? Would they know what to do, or would they find a mess?
- Would you characterize yourself as a wealth builder or a wealth receiver? How did your family talk about money when you were growing up? Did they talk about it at all? If not, why do you think they didn't? Does it make sense?
- Did your parents and grandparents plan ahead for their own passing or for their estate? Did they have wealth? Did everyone get along? How well did they communicate those plans to you?
- How have your life experiences, good or bad, affected your ability to talk with your family about the future?

- Do you have an inventory of your business enterprise or your net worth—even just one sheet of paper? Does your family know where it is located? If not, how does that avoidance affect your future plans?
- Which of the myths do you recognize in your own mindset? Are there others that aren't on the list?
- How often do you talk with your spouse and children about your values, your money, and their future?
- Are there any tensions and communication glitches in your family? Would it help to get an outside facilitator?
- How will your family (not your business partners, not the public) remember you?
- What have you kept silent about with the people who love you the most, particularly as it relates to what you've built?

WISE WORDS

> "And this mess is so big
> And so deep
> And so tall,
> We cannot pick it up
> There is no way at all!"
>
> —*Dr. Seuss, The Cat in the Hat*

STRATEGIC ACTION PLAN

Objective:

Due Date:

Why is it important?

What will be the end result?

Who will be responsible for this project?

Who to contact:

Deadline:

Thoughts/Notes:

CHAPTER TWO

UNDERSTAND YOUR STORY AND SHARE IT

Your history shapes your wealth building journey. Your family needs to understand that journey, and what wealth means to you.

A successful entrepreneur sold his business for more than enough money to keep himself, his wife, and children comfortable for the rest of their lives and beyond. He had a dozen nieces and nephews, who were all young adults. These young folks were very dear to him, and he wanted to do something special for them that Christmas.

Entrepreneurs are often quick starts. They want to take action, get it done, and move on. That's how they think. He wrote a check for $100,000 to each of his nieces and nephews and put it in their Christmas cards.

When they opened their gifts, they were shocked! They were excited. They hugged him and squealed. They wrote him heartfelt thank-you notes.

By the next Christmas, the excitement was gone. Most of the money was gone, too. He was undoubtedly everyone's favorite uncle, but the moment had passed. He never told them the story that was supposed to accompany those checks. He never shared his "why."

Instead of creating a life-changing opportunity, he created a big splash of excitement and attention that soon faded.

Even worse, his own children were shocked to see their cousins receive such a huge gift when they got nothing. Of course, they were in a position to receive a much larger inheritance down the line, but they didn't know what their father had in mind. They were confused. They felt left out and embarrassed. They didn't know how to ask their father about the situation without sounding greedy, so they didn't say anything.

Those unasked questions built up into a palpable tension that hung over every family gathering afterward. The cousins picked up on it. They felt awkward and guilty and didn't speak about the money or how they used it. They were afraid of sparking resentment or causing a rift, but that very fear and silence were the rift.

The joyful occasion that should have brought the family together and created a legacy of generosity, instead pulled that whole generation apart.

This is a sad, cautionary tale of good intentions gone terribly wrong. Fortunately, that's not what really happened! This story is loosely based on a client of mine. He had the idea to give major financial gifts to the younger members of his family, and he also had the wisdom to discuss this plan with his wife and with me.

His wife was the one who initially put on the brakes. She felt that some more communication was important and didn't think it felt right to hand out fat checks to the nieces and nephews without doing anything for their own children. The children's future inheritance wasn't really acknowledged in this grand gesture, and his wife was hesitant to go along with it. After all, a symbol isn't worth much if nobody knows what it means.

I pressed the client a bit. I asked him what he expected them to do with the money. What was the purpose of the gift? The answers lay in his personal story.

YOUR STORY MATTERS

When I sit down with a new client in my role as a financial advisor, my first step is always to spend time getting to know them. I call this my deep-dive due diligence. In order to give that person insightful and effective advice, I need to understand who they are and what motivates them.

I want to hear their story: where they came from, how they grew up, how they got into business, their ups and downs, and how they got to this point in their journey. I ask them about their ambitions and plans, their challenges, and the worries that keep them up at night. Above all, I want to understand their *why*. Why are they in business? Why did they make one choice as opposed to another? Why do they get out of bed in the morning? Why are they talking to me now?

After we discuss their backstory, we can address their values and hopes for the future. We work together to create plans personally tailored for them, instead of relying on cookie-cutter solutions that arrive in template style and might not apply to their situation at all.

You may be tempted to skip over this chapter because you already know your own story. But *do* you? Have you really sat down to consider all the ways that your life experiences have shaped your attitudes about money, your work ethic, your choices in business, your family relationships, your marriage, the way you raised your children, and the way you want to establish your legacy? Honestly, I'd be very surprised if you have. Most entrepreneurs don't because they prefer **doing** to contemplating. Let's face it, most people rarely think about these big questions—they're complicated and uncomfortable. And who has the time?

How well do you understand your own story?

For my client with the Christmas cards, the story was that in his own youth, he missed out on some great business opportunities because he didn't have the resources to take advantage of them. He wanted his extended family to have opportunities that he never had.

That was a great step, but I continued to challenge his thinking. After all, not everyone has entrepreneurship in their DNA. It's a very specific temperament.

We wanted to make sure that his family members would understand and appreciate the purpose of the gift, and that it would create a positive synergy instead of leaving them confused, overwhelmed, or adrift. So I worked with him to craft his intentions for the gift, and his expression of those intentions.

I sat down with him and his wife, and we unpacked their life story: how they grew up in very different backgrounds, how they met at university, and everything they went through to build up the business and their wealth. Then I asked him to articulate three or four lessons that he wanted his nieces and nephews to learn, that would guide them in using this money.

The lessons he chose were to work hard, be honest, and pay it forward. That gave him a great idea: instead of giving each of them a round amount, he'd give them that much plus $1,000. The last thousand was for them to give away to do good. Then they'd all come together the following Christmas to share their stories of what they did with that $1,000. Brilliant—not my idea—theirs, as a result of taking the time to think creatively and collaborate.

At first, their intention was to give their children the same gift, so they wouldn't feel left out. I took a different point of view. What message would his children receive if he merely treated them the same as their cousins? It seemed to me that giving identical gifts would dilute his relationship with his children.

So instead, he decided to talk to his children about their own financial gift, which was much larger. Then they received the letter with the $1,000, so they could all participate in the "pay it forward" project together while still knowing that they were special to their parents. Ultimately, that brought everyone closer together and prompted some wonderful family moments: moments that brought about discussions regarding values, vision, and family.

They were both very excited about the way our collaboration elevated their intention from simply writing a check to creating a meaningful gift. I guarantee that those young people will keep those letters forever. **Instead of a transaction, they created a transformation for the whole family.**

That's a great example of Legacy Thinking. Let's walk you through the same thought process. As you read this chapter, imagine that we're having that conversation together. As I did in the first chapter, I'm going to pose a number of questions. Take the time to consider them and recall the stories that have shaped your life. You'll need that insight in order to move forward.

DISCOVER YOUR STORY

When I have conversations with successful entrepreneurs, I find that most of them came from very humble beginnings, or watched their parents build a business from scratch. We're all the products of our childhood, whether that's poverty, wealth, culture, trauma, success, or any other circumstance. Those life experiences shape us. Maybe you grew up wanting a bigger future. Maybe you came from comfortable beginnings and don't want to lose that standard of living. Wherever we come from, we learn.

Wealth builders who lived through struggles saw and felt the sacrifices that are necessary to create prosperity, whether that's to put food on the table or provide a good education for their children. Witnessing those sacrifices often creates a sense of responsibility to be the very best at what they do, to make the sacrifice worthwhile. Stories about the joy and pride of creating a successful business, achieving your goals, and the personal satisfaction of being an entrepreneur are also important. After all, if being in business is all misery, why would your child even want to be part of it?

Unfortunately, the time and energy that entrepreneurs devote to their business success often leave them less time to devote to their families. When they have family time, they naturally want to enjoy it! They want to focus on their loved ones, on the present and the future, instead of dwelling on the past. It's only natural that they forget to share stories of their past with their children.

However, it's important to remember that knowing where you came from helps you understand who you are and who you can become. Witnessing their parents' and grandparents' struggles and accomplishments gives the younger generation a strong sense of identity and security, as well as adding meaning and purpose to their own lives.

In my life, I can see how personal tragedies helped to set me on a path in life. My mother died when she was just twenty-seven; I was two and a half years old. Her death left my father in a very precarious financial situation, and I grew up with very little. The sense that I needed to be responsible for myself always stayed with me, because I felt that no one was responsible for my future but me—including my postsecondary education, my financial future, and otherwise.

That's exactly what I did. I started babysitting at thirteen or fourteen. I got a job at fifteen, and always worked—sometimes two jobs. Those were tough times, but they made me stronger. They also made me value independence and careful planning. I never wanted to leave my spouse in a position where he would have to work twice as hard if I died. I wanted him to have the choice of how to put his life back together or what to do with his career. I didn't want the person I loved to be in a desperate situation with no options.

My father remarried, and my stepmother (who I always just considered "Mom") had a huge impact on me. Even with her love and encouragement, in the back of my mind, I never thought I'd live to be thirty. When I turned thirty, I still wasn't convinced I'd ever see forty. Again, at forty I never expected to be fifty, but here I am at sixty, looking at all the ways I can help other business owners think long-term and plan for their futures in an intentional way.

Don't be afraid to acknowledge painful memories. They are an important part of your story, too. You aren't alone. One hundred percent of families have baggage, whether from their own parents, life experiences, spouses and children, or all of the above. Even if you and your nuclear family seem to have it all together, think back one or two generations. Think outward to your siblings, your cousins, and your in-laws. Somewhere in there you'll find bad behavior, addiction, major medical or mental health problems. That's a legacy that affects generations with complexity, struggle, and hidden pain.

Family complexity is normal, and it affects you every day. Denial, silence, and shame just make it harder to address. Along with discussing your values and hopes, you also need to be humble and transparent about the unintentional mistakes you may have made, whether in business or in parenting. We are all human and we can't do everything perfectly. We all make mistakes with our kids. But honesty and communication can heal a lot of wounds and go a long way toward reconciling damaged relationships.

How did you get where you are today? It's important to uncover those insights, because they will help you understand how to manage your wealth in an intentional way. When you don't consider your stories or acknowledge and accept your roots, you rob your children of the true essence of your wealth. You rob them of the lessons of your success: the resilience, patience, and courage it takes to wake up every morning and own your day.

THE GAP AND THE GAIN

Discovering your story is also important for you personally. The author Dan Sullivan has great insight into the mindset of entrepreneurs. In his book *The Gap and the Gain*, he describes a phenomenon I've seen over and over again. Business owners, wealth builders, and other successful individuals are forward-looking. Our default setting is to keep our eyes fixed on a goal, to push ourselves to see what we're capable of, and to imagine the impossible.

That focus on the future keeps us moving forward through all sorts of difficulties. It's a powerful force! It can also become unbalanced. We need to take time to look around and practice insight and hindsight, too.

When we start our life journey, we keep our eyes on the horizon and see our big, exciting, boundless future. If you think about it, what happens to the horizon when you travel? It always moves ahead of you. You never reach the horizon; it just keeps spreading out forever.

The same thing happens to our goals as we begin to achieve great things. When we earn a million dollars, we see someone else earning ten million, and our achievement seems small by comparison. When we earn ten million, we see someone else with a billion. There is always a gap between our current position and that infinite horizon, and we stay stuck there in the gap. It's not about comparing ourselves directly to others but seeing how far we could go. Eventually, dwelling in the gap can make us devalue what we've created. We don't stop to take stock of our wealth and our impact on others.

> **There is always a gap between where you are and where you want to go. Don't stay stuck in the gap. Measure your progress by how far you have come.**

Sometimes, we're uncomfortable acknowledging our accomplishments, because that constantly shifting horizon makes us feel that we are capable of so much more. A sense of humility keeps us grounded; however, staying stuck in that never-ending gap contributes to unnecessary stress. We are so excited about future opportunities that we neglect to take a moment to enjoy the present and appreciate the past. It also can distract us from considering the practical aspects of planning effectively for the future.

That's why it's so important to look back at where we started and how far we've come. We need to appreciate all that we've gained. Even the painful trials and struggles, while not pleasant memories, are valuable. Recalling the things we've overcome gives us strength, resilience, and confidence. It also lets us experience gratitude and helps us make connections with others to create a more meaningful life.

When I graduated from McGill University, I had $12 in my bank account. The minimum gift they asked from graduating students that year was $10. I figured I was so broke, what the hell difference did it make? I still vividly remember writing out that check, not knowing where my next dollar was coming from.

Thirty-five years later I think about how lucky I am to be able to write a significantly larger check to support a cause that I believe will help others, without worrying about taking food from my family. That sense of joy and freedom is beyond words.

Whatever your past may be, positive or negative, you learn from it. Those experiences impact your life now, and they can help your children and grandchildren put their own struggles into perspective and provide a source of strength and inspiration. Your stories are nuggets of wisdom and the reflection of your essence. They shaped your values, beliefs, and priorities. In the same way that your struggles give you resilience, they can help your children find courage, too.

There's a saying in Italian: *la bella figura*. It means to put on a nice face, or to keep up a good impression. That often translates to "suck it up, Buttercup." Don't let anyone see that you're vulnerable. Don't tell anyone that you're in pain, or that your mental health is suffering. That principle really resonates in some families (Italian or not), and sometimes that mindset goes too far.

Often the children of those families believe their parents are superheroes. But superheroes have feelings, too. They can cry. They can make mistakes. They can struggle to make the right decision. Your children need to understand your own moments of indecision or doubt, so they can see how you found the inner strength to move forward. They can't develop the same strength if they don't see how much effort it really takes.

When kids don't see their parents' struggles, they feel alone. They can be afraid or ashamed to ask for help because they don't want to let us down. Those pent-up insecurities can drive so many relationship and mental health issues.

When you share your own vulnerabilities and moments of indecision or conflict, your children learn how to overcome their own challenges. When children (and adult children) realize their parents are normal human beings who are trying hard and doing their best, it releases them from a lot of anxiety and feelings of inferiority. We all experience rejection, fear, and failure. Your kids need to know how you worked through it so they can learn to work through their own.

SHARE YOUR STORY

More often than not, the parent is the person who keeps a family together. They are the tree that keeps the branches growing in harmony by managing all the different personalities and interests. When that connection is no longer there, the dynamics change and branches that were growing apart fall away from each other. If your children don't get along, you can't force them to be best friends, but you can foster understanding and make it easy for them to be kind to each other. Don't just assume that they'll figure it out after you die. They—and you—can figure it out together while you're still here.

We can't control how our loved ones think, feel, or behave now, much less after we're gone. However, we have a responsibility to do our best and model healthy, open communication. If that doesn't work, we can at least try not to make the situation any worse. The more intentional you are about having these conversations while you can, the better the odds that your children will be able to keep on communicating well after they lose you.

The gifts you leave for your family extend far beyond anything material or financial. The biggest gifts you have to give are the lessons you learned. I don't know about you, but I'd rather have someone teach me something than give me something. What treasured memories, values, and wisdom did your parents leave you? What life lessons do you want your children and grandchildren to remember? What experiences, good and bad, have shaped you? Where do you draw your inspiration, your drive, and your sense of purpose? What values can you share with your loved ones to help them live a happier, more intentional life?

CREATING CONVERSATIONS

When a family has grown up without engaging in money-oriented conversations, there can be a lot of resistance and inertia to overcome. It's been my privilege to help many families start this process. As the wealth holder, consider what you want to happen in the course of these family discussions, and if you are a business owner, what you want to happen to your enterprise in the long term. At this point, you aren't finalizing a plan or making any binding decisions. You're just sketching out the rough draft of some talking points, so don't try to nail down every detail.

Entrepreneurs are creative, and most of the time they envision a big future, where they provide their kids with more opportunities as their enterprise continues to grow. This strong sense of purpose and desire for growth isn't about greed. It's a kind of scorecard. Driven people constantly want to improve. They're competing with themselves, and they always want to outdo their personal best. There's a saying that a mile of road will take you one mile, but a mile of runway can take you anywhere. Entrepreneurs long to build runways for themselves and their families. Go ahead and dream big!

Next, I encourage you to connect with each family member. Take them out for a cup of coffee or an ice cream. Ask them how they feel about their current circumstances, plans for their future, and their thoughts about money. Sometimes those preliminary discussions are best conducted one-on-one. For other families, it's best to broach the topic when everyone is together in the same room, or even with the help of a facilitator. The ultimate goal of this process is to create conversations with the whole family group, so everyone is on the same page.

PACE YOURSELF

You won't be able to share your whole story or download all of your knowledge and values in a single discussion. It's imperative that you break the pattern of silence and begin a new pattern of deep as well as big-picture conversations. This begins with many small actions that form a habit.

Sometimes I use the analogy that talking with your kids about money is more difficult than talking to them about sex. Sex may be a taboo subject, but eventually that conversation happens, regardless of how embarrassing and awkward it may be. Money conversations are just as important as sex conversations. They will learn about money somewhere—Facebook, Instagram, universities pushing credit cards like candy, and so on. Better that they learn the facts from their parents who love them, instead of picking up all kinds of nonsense out in the world. It's part of your parental responsibility to make sure they get true information and wholesome values. And better that they start learning *before* they're in a situation where they really need it!

Child development experts say that having one big talk about "the birds and the bees" just isn't enough. It's probably too little, too late. Instead, the wisest approach is to have many small, age-appropriate conversations throughout their childhood, as they start to ask questions. Then as they grow, those questions get more complicated, and the answers get more detailed.

Talking about money works the same way. The best way to impart your values and wishes for your children and guide them to becoming stewards of your financial legacy is to start small. Talk about one piece of the puzzle at a time. Don't make it a lecture, but a dialogue. Answer their questions and explain your thinking. Pepper them with stories. Your children want to know you, and that means they want to understand your *why*, too.

> There's a story behind everything we value.

CREATING OPPORTUNITIES

Life is full of good occasions to share your stories with your family, because there's a story behind everything we value. As the matriarch or the patriarch, it's your responsibility to invite your loved ones together. You may feel as if you don't have enough time to prioritize your planning and your family communication but let me challenge your thinking. Do you have time to make a business lunch and build your network? Do you have time for golf with a business colleague, or a celebratory dinner when you close a deal? These family planning sessions are just as important—vital—to the long-term success of your enterprise and your family's well-being.

If you only call your family together to discuss bad news, like a divorce or life-threatening illness, then unfortunately, that's what they'll expect. Other families only get together for happy occasions like Christmas or Thanksgiving, but they don't have deep conversations. You can reset those expectations by including deep family discussions with joyful milestones like holidays and birthdays. If so, make sure to let everyone know that you want to talk about planning for the future. Don't spring a serious discussion on them out of the blue, because people have all kinds of different feelings about these talks. As we discussed in Chapter One, talking about money can be emotionally fraught. Don't blindside anyone. (I speak from experience, as I have often made this mistake, and my children don't appreciate it.)

I usually recommend calling an entirely separate family meeting to discuss legacy planning. The whole point is to be intentional and setting aside time for this purpose can help everyone stay focused. Perhaps you can make them a special event with their own type of celebration. Whatever approach you choose, be intentional about the schedule and the tone, so your loved ones have something to look forward to instead of something to dread. Make sure your planning includes time for their voices to be heard.

GET SUPPORT

If you need a third party to break the ice, I encourage you to find an advisor or facilitator who can help. It's a normal part of our business—or it should be. If you believe the discussion is likely to be tense, there are even family financial therapists who specialize in helping families navigate these issues.

I've had the privilege of being invited to such meetings as an advisor, and sometimes to help kids unpack how they perceive their father or mother. I always start off with something positive, and I recommend you do the same. Share a positive thought, and share an important message, before you dive into the nitty-gritty details. I'll confess that with my own family I tend to jump into the business end with very little preamble, but of course we've been doing family meetings a couple of times a year and discussing money with the kids nearly their whole lives. If these conversations are new to you, take it slow and give plenty of time for everyone to be heard.

GET TOGETHER

Once you break the silence and start having authentic conversations with your family, amazing things happen. Your children and grandchildren will get to know you in a new way and gain new appreciation for everything you've built. You'll also see different sides of them, and hear their perspectives on their own lives, hopes, and dreams.

When you're ready, start planning a family gathering. To ease into serious talks, there are all kinds of resources available to encourage thoughtful, fun conversations around the table. Make these gatherings a habit, and you'll soon find ample opportunities to share the stories your family needs to hear.

I particularly like questions and games that everyone can participate in. Some of my favorites include the card game *Table Topics*, *The Complete Book of Questions: 1,001 Conversation Starters for Any Occasion* by Garry D. Poole, and *If...Questions for the Soul* by Evelyn McFarline and James Saywell.

Sharing your stories will help you all come together and imagine your future. Your family legacy is an amazing opportunity to make an impact on the world. That's what we'll discuss next, as we explore the ways that your values shape your vision.

HOMEWORK

- Where are you from, and how did you grow up? How do you think your early life experiences shaped your feelings about money and family?
- What treasured memories, values, and wisdom did your parents leave you? Where do you draw your inspiration, drive, and sense of purpose?
- How did you get where you are today? Why did you choose your business? Why did you choose your spouse?
- What struggles affected you most as you built your business? How about struggles that affected your family?
- What sacrifices have you made in order to become successful? Are they similar to or different from the sacrifices your parents made?

- What challenges are facing you now? What keeps you up at night?
- What prompted you to read this book right now?
- What outcome would you like to see from sharing your story with your family?
- What would you like to see happen with your business enterprise in the long term?
- What life lessons do you want your children and grandchildren to remember? What values can you share with your loved ones to help them live a happier, more intentional life?

WISE WORDS

> "Life can only be understood backwards;
> but it must be lived forwards."
>
> —*Søren Kierkegaard*

STRATEGIC ACTION PLAN

Objective:

Due Date:

Why is it important?

What will be the end result?

Who will be responsible for this project?

Who to contact:

Deadline:

Thoughts/Notes:

CHAPTER THREE

GIVING WITH PURPOSE

Plan your wealth to include the causes that matter to you.

Imagine a rainstorm pouring down on a residential neighborhood. It's a real gully washer. The soil has already absorbed all that it needs to support the grass and trees. The excess rainwater runs off into the gutters, and they're surging with rushing water. At every point on the street, from every driveway and downspout, hundreds and thousands of gallons of water converge in the storm drain and swirl down into the wastewater system. Everything gets washed down together: leaves, trash, dog poop, car fluids, and all. Eventually, all that water winds up in a reservoir, where it gets filtered, cleaned, treated, and recycled back into the water supply. No matter where a single drop of water falls, it winds up being merged with all the others and reused in service of the community.

Now imagine a house on that same street with rain barrels underneath its roof gutters. The barrels catch a portion of the water that's bucketing down, so the owner can direct it where they want it to go. Instead of flowing down the storm drain indiscriminately, these streams of water have a specific purpose—they may be used to water the owner's garden, wash their car, or splash the grandchildren on a hot summer day. That water will wind up doing many of the same jobs that the runoff water would do. The difference is that the owner made a plan to direct it in a specific, productive, and more efficient way (without all the dog poop). We can't control the rain, but we have the opportunity to direct some of the water.

That flow of water represents your social capital: your investment in the good of society.

When you launch a business, most likely your initial goal is to put food on the table and provide a comfortable lifestyle for your family. Your trajectory of success may be a little bumpy, but in time you may reach a point where your family has all their needs met, they have plenty to enjoy, and their financial future is secure. As a result of your hard work, resilience, and courage, you may have more wealth than you require to support your lifestyle and family.

When you die with wealth, a portion of this wealth must be reinvested in society. This social capital legacy has two parts: taxes and charity. Like the rainwater running off your property, some of that excess wealth is returned to society to help it keep functioning. Some of your estate will have a tax obligation. If you have faith that it will all work out in the long run, you can just let it all flow down the storm drain.

However, with proper planning, some of those tax dollars can be redirected for the benefit of charities—just like putting rain barrels under your roof. Purposeful, planned giving is the epitome of proper estate thinking. It allows you to determine whether the tax obligation goes directly to the government or is transformed and redirected to causes that are important to you.

First, let's unpack what social capital means. Then we'll discuss how your heartfelt values can guide you in building purposeful giving into your estate plan. Finally, we'll examine different ways to direct your giving that create significant impact and transmit your values to future generations.

WHAT IS SOCIAL CAPITAL?

Human capital consists of the work we do and the value we create to build wealth. Social capital consists of the contributions we make to our communities. These two types of capital are interconnected. There is an ebb and flow between creating wealth, giving wealth, and receiving. This reciprocity can extend beyond money, into something as simple as helping a neighbor, or volunteering for a nonprofit or a special cause. Social capital can take many forms, from random acts of kindness, to writing checks to charity, to engaging in civic duties. It comprises all our investments of time, energy, and money to support our communities.

> **Social capital consists of the contributions we make to our communities.**

You give back to society in many ways during your lifetime, particularly as a business owner. Building a successful business creates layers and layers of benefit to the community. Entrepreneurs are the foundation of a strong and vibrant economy and create massive social capital along with their financial capital. They employ people and feed families. Their work creates a financial ripple effect for suppliers, bankers, accountants, lawyers—even the grocery stores where their employees shop. This continuous cycle of money flowing through society creates jobs and other businesses, generates tax revenue, and is amplified with time.

For every significant estate or family enterprise, there will also be a social capital obligation when the wealth builder dies, in the form of estate tax.

TAXES AS SOCIAL CAPITAL

Of course, paying taxes is important. Over your lifetime you've paid a ton: income tax, property tax, business tax, sales tax. You write the check, and it goes into a big vat, and who knows where it might end up? Someone else decides whether that money is going to build a road, protect the environment, provide for the military, support families on welfare—or whether it's simply wasted on bureaucracy.

Those are all important (except bureaucracy)! But wouldn't it be more satisfying if you could determine exactly where these tax dollars were going, and the effect they would have? Even though you've paid taxes your whole life, the big check is yet to be written. Estate taxes can be a hidden bomb to business owners who don't realize the magnitude of the wealth they have created, and how taxes may create illiquidity challenges due to the outstanding tax bill at death. I don't want this to happen to you. Mindfully planning your estate to maximize your social capital means you can redirect a big chunk of that tax obligation toward a cause you know, understand, and support.

Now, if you choose not to make provisions in your planning to direct your tax dollars toward charities (whether grassroots or global), that's perfectly okay. It's your choice. All this means is that the money from your estate taxes will funnel directly to the government, and the government will distribute these dollars (*your* dollars) for you. Some might argue that it's all going toward the public good anyway, so what's the difference?

For starters, our tax dollars support all parts of the government—the ones you agree with, and the ones you don't. Let's face it, a lot of government systems are broken, and fail the people they're supposed to help. For example, you see social workers struggling in an unbelievably tough job. They're underpaid, understaffed, and barely have a fraction of the resources they need to really help people in dire situations. It's overwhelming. On the other hand, you have all these Wall Street types who were paid millions of dollars in bonuses during the 2008 crash—the same guys who were responsible for the crash in the first place! And it was all funded by a massive government bailout—paid with tax money.

In addition, a great many people lack faith in the government's ability to use taxpayer money in an efficient and effective manner. Government has become a labyrinth of departments that don't communicate and are often in conflict with each other. We all have some level of obligation to support good government, though we may want to consider an even larger responsibility: contributing to our communities and society through sound charities that have a direct, positive impact. If you can redirect some of your tax dollars to organizations that you believe will contribute to making a better impact on society, why wouldn't you?

Entrepreneurs are the quintessential problem solvers and solution creators, and you can design solutions for this tax obligation that's due to go down the storm drain. You can choose now to make it work better by directing it toward organizations that will benefit your community.

Wherever you are on your journey today, I encourage you to think ahead. Consider what you'd like to accomplish with your social capital legacy. Where do you want to make a difference? What issues or causes would you like to help with? What changes would you like to see in the world? How do you take some of your **significant** wealth, and transform it into **significance** in your giving?

GIVING AS SOCIAL CAPITAL

The key to creating a vision for your giving is to think deeply about the causes that are important to you and find the common thread that ties them together—those core values that run all the way through your life. Be mindful of your history, your beliefs, and the causes that touch your heart and create impact. This might even be an interesting starting point to have a conversation with your family members and get them involved.

> Think deeply about your values and then think creatively about your estate plan.

There are many reasons people give to charity. Often, a particular cause becomes meaningful to someone because it has touched them in a personal way. Perhaps you have a personal or family connection that prompts you to care for the elderly, youth, the homeless, or families with food insecurity. Perhaps you or someone you love was affected by an addiction, a mental health issue, or a certain disease, and you want to sponsor research in their memory. Perhaps you're excited about providing service dogs to the blind, or to veterans with PTSD. For me, the meaningful connection was part of a personal journey that began when I was a new graduate in my early twenties.

CONNECTING THE DOTS

In those early days of my career, everything was about survival. I was working hard and trying to save money. One day I walked past a homeless man and recalled that a client told me panhandlers make a lot of money because so many people give to them automatically. I pretended not to see and walked right past this guy—and many others like him.

I was ambitious, hardworking and a meticulous planner. My goal was to be financially independent. I knew if I worked hard, was honest and open to learning, I had a big future. I truly believed that this guy was homeless because he had a terrible plan, or no plan at all. In my mind, this man's complex situation was reduced to his lack of a plan, so I dismissed him.

Later, about six years into my practice, I was working in overdrive. Business and family demands were colliding, and I needed a breather. I saw an article about the wilderness program Outward Bound. I was intrigued, because I'd grown up a city girl and never experienced camping or had many outdoor adventures. I signed up for their women's empowerment course.

The trip itself was a wonderful experience in a beautiful provincial park in Ontario. We were a whole group of women from different backgrounds and circumstances. We paddled the rivers, portaged our canoes, hiked and camped, sat by evening fires to chat about life amid a sprinkling of activities to foster communication and build trust. As the women in the group opened up, my eyes were opened to some of the harsh realities that they'd grown up with, and how their lives were shaped by those traumas. It was humbling to hear all the ways that this course was a major life achievement for some of them and helped them make breakthroughs in their self-confidence and courage. I just went because I'd never shit in the woods!

Being a planner, I'd been preparing for this trip for months. I hit the gym every day and got in the best shape of my life. One young woman, Sue, seemed completely unprepared. She was very overweight, out of shape, and out of place. She obviously hadn't done any planning or preparation. I wasn't sure how she could manage the physical challenges of the expedition at all.

It turned out that Sue lived in my city, so I offered her a ride home on the last day. During the drive, she told me her life story. Her father was a very successful professional and also very abusive. She had no protection from predatory boys and experienced sexual assault. The family had no stability and moved around frequently. Her mother left and came back several times. Eventually, Sue ran away from home. She found a boyfriend and got pregnant. He beat her so badly that she miscarried. The story went on, and her life was full of one trauma after another, up to the point that her mother had gifted her this Outward Bound trip.

I don't know how long I drove with my mouth hanging open. Suddenly, I saw her in a completely different light. I told her, "Sue, you're the first woman I've ever met that's been abused by a man."

She replied, "Sandy, you're the first woman I've ever met that's *never* been abused by a man."

This was a turning point in my life. For the first time, it made me realize—in a very concrete way—that what you see on the surface of someone's life isn't necessarily the whole picture. It's just the tip of the iceberg, and you have no idea what might be going on underneath. What you see is only a fraction of what remains to be seen.

I was wrong to be so judgmental and brash, not just toward

Sue but toward the homeless person that I had seen on the street and probably most everyone I encountered. After all, Sue's dad was a well-known person in the community—the last person I would imagine as abusive. I was so focused on getting ahead in my own life that it blinded me to the human beings around me who needed understanding and compassion. That encounter with Sue, and with myself, was beyond enlightening. It was transformative. It made me realize that my own problems and accomplishments are insignificant in themselves, but I could make a significant difference in someone else's world. It also made me realize that everyone has a story, and not all stories are simple or pretty.

This shift in my thinking caused a ripple effect in my life. It clarified my values and realigned my mindset. It widened my perspective on the world around me. I came to learn that it is our responsibility to care for those less fortunate, and to do so without judgment, because we are not privy to a person's real story until we truly take the time to listen and understand.

Years later, a charity that served the homeless made a presentation to a community foundation whose board I sat on. At the end of the presentation, they invited anyone who might be interested to join them on their walks. That walk was the most eye-opening experience of my life, and it moved me to make a long-term commitment as a volunteer helping the homeless. We distribute food and warm clothing, and we help connect people on the streets with resources if they're willing. Sometimes, the most important thing we offer is companionship. No matter how terrible a person's circumstances may be, they just want to be treated like a human being. We talk to them, ask how they're doing, and even get to know some regulars.

This experience has been and continues to be so meaningful to me. For one thing, if I could collect all the "God bless yous" that these folks give, I'd be in heaven for sure. Beyond that, I get to see these people who are destitute—who have absolutely nothing—turn around and exercise generosity. So often, I've seen someone receive something, like a pair of socks, and then give it to another person because they think that another person needs them more. These experiences are grounding, and often keep me from losing my head when dealing with money and affluence in my work. It amplifies the importance of looking beyond one's own comfort to truly see the disparity of wealth and participate in projects that do good for the community.

Over the years, my husband and I have created a small foundation with the assistance of a community foundation, and the investment income on that capital goes toward this particular program. This foundation will continue after we're gone.

As you formulate your vision for giving, think deeply about your values and then think creatively about your estate plan. There are many different approaches to leverage your planning in a tax efficient way to multiply the positive effects of the wealth you created. Be sure to discuss your values and choices with your family. Those discussions can be very enlightening and show them how your money can do good things in society.

ANONYMITY AND LEADERSHIP

In my faith tradition, we believe in the principle of *tzedakah*, the moral obligation to give to those in need, which is an integral part of *tikkun olam*, repairing the world. We are responsible for leaving this world better than we found it and giving to charity is one of the many ways to accomplish that. There's a strong belief that giving quietly and humbly is true giving. There are many wealth holders who give generously—and anonymously—to charities that are meaningful to them. They might write checks for $10,000 or $100,000 or more, but never tell their children about this support, or why they have chosen that particular cause or organization. This gesture of humility is a beautiful, precious thing!

The only caveat is that, as we discussed in Chapter One, silence has a price. If you choose not to share the "how" and "why" behind your giving with your family, it may stop the flow of financial generosity for future generations. Sharing your purpose with your loved ones can turn your gifts today into a seed that provides abundance in the future. I encourage you to take your family into your confidence about your quiet giving, even if the donation is anonymous to the rest of the world. Having conversations with your children about how and why you give is often the forgotten piece of the family legacy puzzle. Taking it one step further, your children may even have their own causes that ignite their giving. These family conversations can build a sense of responsibility to be generous in their own lives and more often than not create stronger family relationships.

Leadership in giving is also very important. When a leader in the community is seen giving a lot, it provides an example and can inspire or encourage others who might not have considered giving. Your gift can have an even greater impact by multiplying gifts from others. These two sides of the coin—anonymity and leadership—work together to ensure the fabric of our communities stays strong. Finding that balance between privacy and leadership is a personal decision for each individual.

Do your children and grandchildren know about the causes you support? How have you modeled community involvement, volunteering, and generosity for them? Are there ways you could get them more involved, or create teachable moments to discuss the importance of giving? Perhaps there are causes that they care about that you could include in your giving program.

CHOOSING WHERE AND HOW TO GIVE

You may be looking for the right organization to support with a significant donation and need direction to clarify all available options for giving. In Canada, there are three ways to donate to registered charities: through private foundations, through public foundations that specialize in donor-advised funds, or direct to the nonprofit itself.

> Make sure the charitable giving in your estate plan is intentional, reflects your values, and is set up properly through your advisors.

PRIVATE FOUNDATIONS (AKA PRIVATE FAMILY FOUNDATIONS)

If you have a strong desire for control and involvement with the administration and investments of your charitable capital, you could start your own foundation and appoint your family, colleagues, or advisors to the board. This is a complex process with a number of drawbacks.

There are extensive compliance requirements for private foundations. Your mandate and recordkeeping must be clear and precise, and they become subject to public scrutiny. The foundation must be approved by the government and the minutes and other records must be audited regularly. This administrative load takes a great deal of time and may detract from your focus on giving.

Setting up such a foundation requires specialized legal and tax advice. Often, these professional fees will eat into the capital you have available to invest. This option is usually recommended only if you have an initial gift greater than $10 million.

PUBLIC FOUNDATIONS (AKA DONOR-ADVISED FUNDS)

Public foundations are umbrella organizations that meet the regulatory requirements for registered charities, and which enable individuals to donate capital and then direct the investment income earned to charities of their choice. The administrative fees are usually significantly less than for a private foundation, because of the economies of scale. The initial investment to start a donor-advised fund can be as low as $5,000.

The foundation administers the compliance, reporting, bookkeeping, investment policy statements, disbursements, and other day-to-day management functions. They also handle the reporting and tax receipts. Altogether, the foundation manages the "what" and "how" of running a charity. That leaves donors free to focus on the "who" and "why" of their giving. It also creates a level of anonymity, as the size of your fund can remain private if you so desire.

DIRECT TO NONPROFITS

Sometimes finding the right charity to support is like fishing in the ocean. It is so vast; how do you choose? Industry statistics show that there are more than 170,000 registered nonprofits in Canada, and more than 1.5 million in the US. There are grassroots organizations that serve the needs of your community locally, as well as larger nonprofits like the Canadian Cancer Foundation. With all those organizations to choose from, how do you discern whether a charity is really making a positive impact, or whether they're just creating employment for their executives?

If you give money directly to a nonprofit organization, you want to be certain that they are accomplishing their mission, whether that's feeding the hungry, supporting the arts, advancing medical research, or whatever the case may be. I know that some people are deeply suspicious of nonprofits, and not entirely without reason! There have been a number of high-profile scandals in recent years that could make anyone think twice about how their donations are being used (or not).

For example, in the summer of 2020 the Canadian government announced that the Canada Student Service Grant program would offer a substantial stipend, up to $5,000, for students who volunteered to serve their communities. This program would be administered by the nonprofit WE Charity. Supposedly, this organization had been vetted by the Public Service and chosen as the only possible option. It turned out that they were the only organization that had been invited to submit a proposal, and the grant was awarded in a no-bid deal conducted behind closed doors. Throughout the rest of 2020 and into 2021, a massive conflict-of-interest investigation ensued that embroiled both the Prime Minister and the Finance Minister in allegations of cronyism and ethics violations.

The annual reports of registered charities are publicly available, and I recommend you read them to ensure your chosen charity is achieving its stated purpose. Nonprofit ratings groups like Charity-Watch.org can also give you in-depth information, analysis, and quality ratings on national and international organizations to help you assess where your donations might be put to best use. (CharityWatch replaced WE Charity's star rating with a "?" in 2021.) Whenever you choose an organization to support, make sure they are well-managed and accountable.

OTHER GIFTING OPTIONS

There are a number of options for supporting your chosen causes that go beyond making charitable bequests or working through a foundation. It's important to consider other ways to give, beyond cash. Donations can also be made in-kind through stocks, with real estate, or with cryptocurrency. An interesting option is to take out a life insurance policy with the charity as the beneficiary. That can be extremely helpful, because it creates immediate liquidity upon death and may be eligible for tax credits. You could also assign the policy to the charity while you're living, which would result in your premium payments becoming a charitable donation that generates a tax receipt. (Speak to your financial advisor before implementing this option to ensure it's done correctly.)

In Canada, flow-through shares can be used to give large charitable donations at a small net cost. Purchasing shares in certain mining, energy exploration, and renewable energy companies creates a tax incentive that offsets most of the cost of purchase. The Flow-Through Share Donation structure (FTSD) allows donors to transfer the shares to a charity by paying only the transaction costs and a nominal fee, while the charity sells the shares for close to their full value. In practical terms, an FTSD donation of $100,000 might only cost the donor $13,000 after taxes.

No matter what approach you choose, make sure the charitable giving in your estate plan is intentional, reflects your values, and is set up properly through your advisors. Thoughtful planning can carry your vision on a trajectory that broadens your reach and sustains your impact beyond your lifetime for many generations to come.

PURPOSEFUL PREPARATION

As I write this book, the world is going through immense social and economic upheaval due to the COVID-19 pandemic. The disparity between rich and poor is widening, the middle class is disappearing, and the number of people in dire straits has multiplied. Those of us who have been blessed with good fortune have the opportunity to use a sliver of that good fortune to help others, and the need is greater than ever. Use the homework questions at the end of this chapter to consider the causes that matter to you, and how your giving could make a major, enduring impact on them.

As we walk through this book, I want you to see how each stage builds upon everything that came before. First, you must be willing to break through the wall of silence. Then you begin to share your stories. Those stories help you understand and articulate your values and become purposeful in deploying social capital and including family members in the conversation. This deepens your communication with your family, so they understand the legacy you built for them. Next, we'll examine how you can prepare your family to become good stewards of your family business enterprise.

✏ HOMEWORK

- If someone gave you a million dollars with the stipulation that you had to give it away to charity, what three charities would you choose? Why?

- What are the top three causes that you feel led to support with your time and money? Why? Do you already have relationships with organizations that serve those needs?

- If not, how can you use word-of-mouth connections, community resources, and research to find the right recipient for your social capital?

- If you currently support certain charities, why are those organizations meaningful to you? Have you shared these thoughts with your family?

- Do your children know the extent of your charitable giving? Are there direct or indirect ways that you could bring up the subject?

- How could you invite them to join you in serving or supporting these organizations?

- Have you made any charitable bequests in your will? Have you discussed those provisions with your accountant, your lawyer, and most importantly, your family?

- What strategies could you use to maximize the benefit of your giving?

- Review your net worth with an eye to your tax liability. How could you redirect those tax dollars to make a social or community impact?

> **WISE WORDS**
>
> "Service to others is the rent you pay for your room here on earth."
>
> —*Muhammad Ali*

STRATEGIC ACTION PLAN

Objective:

Due Date:

Why is it important?

What will be the end result?

Who will be responsible for this project?

Who to contact:

Deadline:

Thoughts/Notes:

CHAPTER FOUR

A LEGACY OF STEWARDSHIP

Your complex family enterprise is a responsibility. Prepare your family to understand and become stewards of wealth.

Once upon a time, a prosperous business owner had three children. He loved his family and wanted to make sure that the business would provide for their needs. He put his sons on the payroll and gave them seniority according to their personal financial needs. The eldest had two children and was paid well. The middle son had three children, so the business owner paid him more. The youngest had no children yet, so he was paid the least—until he bought a new house and took on a big mortgage, whereupon he was rewarded with a large raise. This system did not endear the sons to each other, or to the other employees.

The owner wanted his children to feel important to the business, so he gave each of them the title of President, regardless of their job skills or contribution to the business. The President of Shipping was particularly proud of the title on his business card. None of them knew how the company as a whole operated. None of them could even read a financial statement.

One day, the owner's wife died of a sudden illness. He was bereft and despondent, and for many months the business was the last thing on his mind. The three sons stepped in, but they had never held a job outside the family business, and they didn't have the same relationships with their father's advisors. They didn't even have the authority to sign checks. They relied on the loyal staff to keep the company going, but had no idea how to supervise them, nor any understanding of proper business management.

None of them realized that the company controller was not an honest man. Given full authority over the business's finances without oversight, he took advantage of the situation to enrich himself with the company's money.

While trying to cope with his tragic and devastating loss, the owner quickly found solace in another woman and married her. As a standard business precaution, when he bought a new house, he put it in his second wife's name to protect it from his business creditors.

Unbeknownst to them all, the controller had created a second set of books and embezzled large sums from the business—right under the sons' noses. When this finally came to light, the bank decided that the business was a bad credit risk. They called in all their loans at once.

The owner lost everything—the business, his retirement, all his savings, and his reputation. He even lost his new wife, who had married him for the money he no longer had. Of course, the house was in her name, so she took it with her. He was penniless.

His pride in his work and in his children blinded him to reality. Willful blindness is human nature, and this father was no exception. He refused to acknowledge his children's lack of management and leadership skills. As a result, he forgot to teach them and mentor them so that they could one day assume responsibility for the business and help it continue to flourish. He forgot to hold them accountable for their mistakes, so they could learn and grow. He had unintentionally given a position of great authority and no oversight to a person who lacked integrity. Without any clear rules of engagement or a defined path to grow, his sons wound up thrust into positions they couldn't handle, like a kindergartner put in the driver's seat when they can't even reach the pedals.

In our story, the owner of that company expected a lot from his sons. He expected them to take over and run the business (though he never even asked whether they wanted to). He expected them to make it grow. He expected them to exercise good stewardship: principled, responsible management (even when he wasn't practicing it himself). He expected them to run the business well, without any training or an instruction manual.

He had expectations, but no plans. In order to bring those expectations into reality, he needed to prepare his children and provide for an orderly business transition. How? By taking the time and engaging the right people to identify the reasons for the success of his business and prepare a roadmap for his children. The components of this roadmap range from financial literacy and family business rules to personal coaching and support from outside.

Your family needs the same preparation. Your complex family enterprise is a big responsibility, and your family needs to be equipped with the right tools to understand, manage, grow, and protect their legacy. To that end, let's take a look at the way family business enterprises flourish, how that creates complexity, and how you can prepare your children to manage intergenerational wealth.

THE CHALLENGE OF A COMPLEX FAMILY ENTERPRISE

Nearly all my family business clients follow a similar path as they grow their enterprises. They start from very little, and as their business grows and becomes profitable, different opportunities present themselves. They expand into other related business ventures, either vertically or horizontally.

For example, a business owner in the construction industry might expand vertically by purchasing another business that was their supplier, like an HVAC company or a lumberyard. Real estate is a common horizontal expansion. At first the entrepreneur might purchase a building to house the company, then lease out part of the space. Then perhaps they might buy land and develop it for another source of income from residential or commercial leasing, as diverse income streams are prevalent in family enterprises. The assets appreciate in value, and as the mortgage gets paid, positive cash flow contributes to his overall wealth. In this way, one successful business can seed a much larger and more complex enterprise.

Many entrepreneurs derive great fulfillment and energy from taking on new opportunities as they grow their wealth. This spirit of adventure can fuel exponential growth. Even when some ideas don't work, they have this amazing mindset that looks back and considers them to be life lessons. They don't dwell on the past because they're always moving forward. I like to call these bumps in the road "pearls of wisdom."

There's a saying that it's hard to read the label when you're sitting inside the jar, and that's the position many successful entrepreneurs find themselves in. It's rare for owners to take a step back and really look at the full scope of what they've built. However, in order to prepare your family to become stewards of their wealth, participate meaningfully in the business, and someday take responsibility for it, you absolutely need to gain that larger perspective.

In addition, too many entrepreneurs are uncomfortable navigating the deep waters of family relationships, required mentorship, and the complex conversations that need to happen, so they neglect to address them at all. Why? Because they're too busy managing their businesses and the everyday problems they need to solve. That's their zone of excellence. They know that preparing their children to be good stewards of their legacy requires a great deal of time, thought, and care, so they place this responsibility gently at the bottom of their to-do list, which most often fails to get done. It's easier to keep putting out the daily fires of managing their enterprise. Unfortunately, those family needs and relationships are smoldering behind their backs all along.

In the last three chapters, you spent a lot of time considering your values and the history of your business. Now look at your current holdings and connect the dots. What guiding principles have led you to take the opportunities you chose? How has the current structure of your enterprise evolved with your acquired life experiences? What are the failures or learning opportunities that happened along the way to get you from there to here? How does it express your priorities and values? Have you taken the time to share those stories and principles with your children? Above all, do your children understand those life experiences and share your priorities?

LEGACY OR LOTTERY?

If your goal is to leave your children and grandchildren a legacy, then they need to be prepared to receive it. Heirs who don't know what to expect or lack a foundation of sound financial skills might as well have won the Lotto. They're stunned, ill-prepared, and rudderless. Unaccustomed to the responsibility and skill set required to manage a multimillion-dollar legacy, and overwhelmed by their new responsibilities, there's a big risk that they may fall victim to poor decisions and other people's greed. The magnitude of this gift is like handing a twelve-year-old the keys to a Lamborghini. The old saying that families go from shirtsleeves to shirtsleeves in three generations reflects the difficulty of maintaining a family business legacy without sound preparation.

Even when they knew a significant legacy would come to them, the second or third generation can sometimes struggle with feelings of guilt or shame that they didn't earn what they have. Many parents worry about spoiling their children and are uncertain how to prepare them properly for wealth, but sometimes that can go too far and cause unintentional problems. Feelings of guilt and shame set the stage for unhealthy relationships and terrible decisions that can be made out of emotion, instead of level-headed reflection. Such choices can have permanent consequences that reverberate through multiple generations.

A DISASTER IN THE MAKING

I was once hired (briefly) by a couple who had seven grown kids. One of them had a terrible problem with opiate addiction after a painful back surgery. She was unable to hold down a job and became completely financially dependent on her parents. The dad simply refused to acknowledge the problem and kept on enabling his daughter. We needed to do their estate plan, and it was just awful because all these problems hung over the conversation: how to deal with the kid, how the situation had impacted the other siblings, whether and how much to provide for them in the future. We couldn't address anything realistically because the husband was in denial. They needed insurance, they had tax issues, and ultimately this inability to communicate honestly made them miserable with each other. The siblings were well aware of the situation. However, they were so busy with their own young families that they chose to tiptoe around the situation and remain silent.

Then the father, the wealth holder, as a result of a substantial business sale, decided to take $5.6 million and split it evenly between the kids, giving it to them free and clear. To him, it was a great idea because he could take advantage of a capital gains tax exemption and pass this money to the next generation tax-free. Did he explain where the money came from, in the long years of building up the business? Did he share the responsibilities that come with significant amounts of money? Did he explain the purpose of these gifts to the recipients? No. Nada. All he did was sign the checks.

So, you tell me—did this gift benefit them or their relationship in the long run? Well, the money was used, but there was no connection to this being a legacy of hard work and sacrifice. There was no guidance on how it should be used. Some of the kids used the money well, but as you can imagine a gift in the hands of someone with such severe addiction didn't do them any good—nor did it improve their relationship with their siblings. The daughter who was struggling didn't get the help she needed. It got to the point that I simply couldn't help this family, and all my advice and recommendations for family meetings, along with gentle noodge-ing, got us nowhere.

Some people make mistakes by giving too much, others by giving too little. Sometimes they make the mistake of never giving anything, including an explanation. So, eventually when the wealth builder dies, the kids wind up in a mess with an inheritance they didn't expect and don't know how to manage.

A TALE OF TWO FORTUNES

Nothing illustrates the difference between a legacy and a lottery more clearly than the contrast between the Rockefeller and Vanderbilt family fortunes.

John D. Rockefeller founded Standard Oil in 1870 and became America's first billionaire. He founded the University of Chicago, and over his lifetime and his children's, the family gave away more than $1 billion. Through ups and downs, each generation has maintained and grown the family fortune while practicing radical generosity. Today, the total assets of the family are approximately $8.4 billion. David Rockefeller, Jr. has stated in interviews that the family cohesion and success are based on clear, consistent teaching of values from one generation to the next. Those principles are summed up in the personal motto of John Rockefeller, Jr.: "For every right implies a responsibility; every opportunity, an obligation; every possession, a duty." The Rockefeller fortune has lasted seven generations, and it's still going strong.

The story of the Vanderbilts could not be more different. In 1877, Cornelius Vanderbilt left $100 million to his family—the largest fortune ever seen in the US up to that point. By the time his son Billy died eight years later, he'd doubled it. Over the years, the family became notorious for reckless spending, drunken revelry, nasty public divorces, and lavish homes they couldn't maintain. According to one of their well-known descendants, journalist Anderson Cooper, he was earning his own pocket money by age thirteen, and lending money to his mother Gloria Vanderbilt not long after. Instead of stewards, they were spendthrifts.

A significant inheritance, just like a windfall, is a huge transition in someone's life that takes time to process. I always advise beneficiaries to tuck their bequests away for six to twelve months to reflect on it. Studies show that people who receive an unexpected windfall (like an inheritance or lottery win) save an average of just 16 cents on the dollar, and about one-third of lottery winners go bankrupt.

Nobody wants to do that to their family. It may not be intentional, but it's too late to tell your children what you meant when you're in a box six feet underground. Don't leave your family in that position. Prepare them for their legacy.

TEACHING FINANCIAL LITERACY AND BUSINESS MANAGEMENT

Would you put your child in the driver's seat of a car for the first time without pointing out where the gas, the brake, the mirrors, and the gearshift are? How well would you expect them to drive with no lessons? In the same way, your children and grandchildren need to learn about money by starting with the basics.

STAGE 1: FINANCIAL LITERACY.

Teach your children about spending, saving, and sharing (not necessarily in that order). This process helps them learn about delayed gratification and goal setting. Encourage them to be curious, practice trial and error, and learn from their mistakes. Praise them for asking questions and reassure them that the only dumb question is the one you didn't ask.

This is an extension of the money lessons we teach our very young children—for example, if they get ten dollars and run to spend it on a cheap toy at the dollar store, is that more or less satisfying than saving it for a video game that will give them hours of entertainment? As they grow, help them gain the knowledge and confidence to make good choices with their own money. For example, they need to understand the good and bad of debt management (like mortgages and credit cards), investing, and income taxes. Money management is a journey through life, from childhood through adolescence to adulthood. After all, if they have never had the experience of managing their own finances, how can they manage a business, or even begin to learn?

When your children have grasped basic financial literacy skills of everyday living, only then is it time to take them a step further, so that you can share and explain some of the specific provisions of your estate plan. What do you have in place, why did you choose it, and what is the purpose of this decision or decisions? As for insurance, why did you choose this type of policy, and how does it function in the overall plan? For example, many successful wealth holders use life insurance as an inexpensive solution to fund estate taxes upon death, because the cost can be as little as thirty cents for every dollar of tax that your estate owes. If you're using any type of trusts in your planning, what is their purpose, what is its impact on them, how did you reach this decision, and why? It's amazing how many successful business owners have little understanding of trusts and other planning structures. As they say, when you teach, you learn!

STAGE 2: BUSINESS MANAGEMENT

Understanding your children's desires and ambitions is critical to find out if they want to become entrepreneurs and have the drive to see it through. Sometimes that desire may present itself later in their young adulthood, when they've gained work experience in other occupations. Sometimes that journey of going out into the world to gain other experiences is an important part of their personal growth and can enrich the family enterprise. If your goal is to have your children continue your business, ensure that this is an invitation, not an obligation. I also recommend that the invitation be conditional on earning the right to become a business owner through certain criteria, such as education or outside experience. This needs to be clearly defined and communicated. When your children are interested, committed, and eager to learn, you can train them in the skills they need to be good stewards of a business, whether that's managing your family business, or managing a new enterprise of their own.

The biggest gift you can give your children and grandchildren isn't money. It's the ability to stand on their own two feet and be productive, caring, self-reliant citizens. In Chapter Three I talked about teaching values in a series of many smaller conversations, instead of trying to do so in one big lecture. In the same way, you should teach your children good financial habits throughout their lives. Money is a renewable resource. As children gain confidence and skills to manage their money, they learn to appreciate it, and the values that form the foundation of wealth.

A mindset of gratitude is foremost among these values. Every entrepreneur that I have worked with—and I have worked with quite a few—shared with how they started, the failures they experienced, the people who helped them along the way. They did not achieve success on their own. All along the way, people helped them. That may be employees, professional advisors, mentors, bankers who gave them a chance, partners who supported you, family who rooted for you, or investors and clients who trusted you.

Acknowledging that support and expressing your gratitude to the people who helped you models gratitude and resilience for your children. Witnessing a mindset of gratitude and abundance growing up will instill that same attitude in them. There's a saying that to teach, you must "tell, show, tell." Powerful stories of times in your own life when you needed help will illustrate that true success is the result of teamwork.

When they understand that you relied on so many others to get where you are, they will learn to work with people, ask for help, and express gratitude, too. This debunks the myth that the business owner did everything on their own—which can often create anxiety and stress for their children who struggle to live up to that impossible standard.

MONEY LESSONS

When your children are old enough to work, they need to learn about saving, sharing, taxes, investing, and responsible spending. One time, we were driving somewhere in our old Honda van. Our middle child said, "I don't get it. Dad's a doctor, you're a financial advisor. We live in a nice neighborhood, and we go to a good school. Why are you talking about how much money things cost all the time? Why are we riding around in this crummy minivan when you could afford nicer cars?"

"That's a good question," I replied. "Your dad and I work really hard, and we have a few different choices as to how we spend our money. We can save some of the money we earn for our retirement, live within our means to put you and your siblings through school, and take vacations we can afford. Or we could spend everything we make on our lifestyle, and then when we are old, we can come and live with you and your family."

You could see the thought bubble over his head. "Save your money," was his reply. I guess the vision of having us with him in his adulthood was too much to digest.

I don't know if he remembers that conversation, but I still get a chuckle out of it. I think at least the principle must have stuck, because now that he's grown, he conscientiously lives within his means and saves for the future. He's so good with money that we tease him about how frugal and careful he is. He chooses to only buy quality items that last and is environmentally conscious of reducing waste by not buying cheap disposable products.

TRANSPARENCY AND EQUITY

We're also very transparent in communicating with all our children, so when we lend or give money to one of them, the others get an equivalent and appropriate amount of help—though not necessarily at the same time. This prevents misunderstandings. There are no secrets between us about loans, gifts, or other financial help. The playing field is clear and even because our ultimate goal is preserving family harmony while we are alive and after we're gone.

Your children are different people, with different needs and goals. Handing out identical dollar amounts isn't necessarily the best way to show them all the same support. For example, we have an old Subaru that we decided to replace. First, we offered it to our eldest daughter. She didn't like it—she wanted to choose a used car on her own. Our son isn't picky about what he drives, and he was happy and grateful to have it.

We wanted to make sure to be evenhanded with our kids, so we gave the eldest a gift equal to the value of that old Subaru. It wasn't much, but she was able to add to her savings and buy the car she really wanted with her own hard-earned money.

Our youngest doesn't need or want a car yet, so we assured her that we'd also help her the same way when she needs it. After all, helping your child financially needs to be based on needs, not wants. The point is that we didn't give them all exactly the same thing at the same time, but we gave them (or will give them) similar amounts of help. We also do our best to have money conversations frequently, so there's clarity. This commitment to transparency and open communication makes all the difference in avoiding the appearance of favoritism.

Money conversations are sometimes difficult for those who have never had them growing up. There is a stigma about talking about money (even though people do talk about it.) The question is, do you want to have these conversations while you are alive in order to teach good money scripts, or leave it to destiny? The problem is, you never know how a child (even an adult child) is going to interpret your actions, or which events they will see and remember. You can't leave it to chance.

I see it in my practice over and over again. A parent dies, there's a disagreement over the estate, and suddenly a grown man regresses to eight years old, complaining that he mowed the lawn every week, but his brother never took out the garbage like he was supposed to. On the surface it sounds ridiculous, but these petty complaints are a symptom of longstanding issues. If one kid feels ignored or neglected as a child, these feelings can be amplified in adulthood, especially if there's a crisis. The latent emotional baggage that they have been carrying around can surface years or decades later in disputes over money. Communication is imperative. One can never over-communicate.

THE FUTURE IS BRIGHT

Perhaps you're looking back and questioning the way you taught your kids about money, or about the choices you made in overindulging them without requiring them to have ownership or accountability. Maybe you have young adults who haven't yet learned to be independent, or who are not making good decisions with their money.

> It's never too late to have productive conversations about money with your family.

It's not too late to reset those boundaries in a healthy way. Indeed, it's never too late to have productive conversations about money, as long as those conversations are accompanied by values and family history and sprinkled with a few interesting stories.

First, I encourage you to take responsibility for your own past decisions, both good and bad. Be kind to yourself and commit to steering a new path of empathy, communication, and responsibility. After all, kids don't spoil themselves. It takes courage and humility to have honest conversations about the relationship and expectations that you built, and why they are or aren't good. I believe anyone can do this, particularly entrepreneurs, because entrepreneurs are the bravest people I know, and they aren't too proud to roll up their sleeves and have hard conversations.

You can start by admitting that you may have messed up on a few things in teaching them about money and wealth building, and that you think the family needs a reboot. Call a family meeting, to discuss the past and the changes that need to be made. Talk about how it's time they started learning to manage their own affairs and weaning off the family accounts so they can gain confidence and become their own person. Don't be capricious or unreasonable but be firm and intentional. Your children deserve the best tools to navigate life, personally, emotionally, and financially. They need independence so they can grow into greater responsibilities, so you need to talk about how they'll manage it.

Be encouraging and supportive. They need to take ownership of their finances, take some risks, and accept hard realities. Young people need to learn by making mistakes and recovering from them, as this is often more valuable than always having everything work in their favor. It's not easy, but it's necessary for them to reach a healthy adulthood and become confident, self-reliant people.

TRAINING STEWARDSHIP SKILLS

I see many successful business owners go wrong when they simply bring their children into the business with the blanket assumption that "someday, all this will be yours." Well, what is **this**? Is **this** the headaches, negativity, problems, and complaints, or is **this** all the nice cars, fancy holidays, nice "stuff," and lots of money?

More often than not, the second generation focuses on one or the other and doesn't grasp that the two sides go together. Sometimes the second generation sees all the problems, and doesn't want to join the business, because they don't want to deal with those issues. Other adult children assume that **this** means the material wealth, ignoring the effort it takes to generate that wealth. This misalignment of success and wealth happens more often than you think.

Instead, "all this will be yours" means the founder wants to pass on both aspects: the wealth they've built, and the hard work, integrity, and dedication it took to create it. They want their children to earn the right to sit at the table. This is often where communication begins to erode, due to these different interpretations and expectations.

When we talk about family legacy or stewardship, it's crucial that you have frank conversations about expectations for involvement in the business—your expectations and theirs. Those conversations should include stories about your own struggle to build the business and keep it growing successfully.

As we discussed in Chapter Two, when children grow up without hearing about any of their parents' wins and losses, failures, risks, fears, and hardships, they often form unrealistic expectations about business ownership. They believe that success comes easily, and that their own success will be automatic. They need to understand the sleepless nights, mistakes that were made, the moments of anxiety and doubt, and the cost of perseverance. You may have tried to protect your family from this stress and aggravation, but how else can they appreciate the depth of everything you built? These deep discussions will help them understand that their family enterprise was built with a lot of risk and sweat equity and instill a sense of pride.

Remember, a conversation isn't a monologue! You also need to listen to your children's hopes and aspirations. Those might include a new and different perspective on the family business. They might not become involved in the family business, or be interested in business at all, but choose a completely different trajectory. Good communication is paramount, and healthy discussions about goals, stewardship, and values require mutual respect and an open mind.

Out of these conversations you can develop a plan for your children to learn the business skills they will need. That plan needs to include defining their roles, giving them clear rules and expectations, and providing them with sound mentors to guide them. Specialists in family business enterprise—objective third-party facilitators experienced in family dynamics, communication, and governance—will be integral to avoiding misalignment of roles and miscommunication.

TWO ROLES FOR YOUR CHILDREN

There are two positions that your children and grandchildren might take in relationship to your business enterprise: employees or passive shareholders. Renato Tagiuri and John Davis at Harvard Business School developed the concept of the three-circle model of family business, now taught as a fundamental principle for family business advisors. Advisors use this model to help business owners understand the inherent conflicts in a family business, and how to manage those conflicts in a productive and healthy manner. The model is shown as a Venn diagram with three circles: Ownership, Family, and Business. Each group has both individual and overlapping concerns and goals.

THREE CIRCLE MODEL
OF THE FAMILY BUSINESS SYSTEM

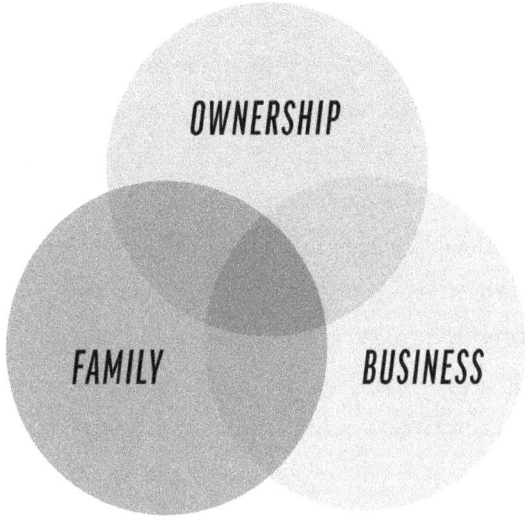

FAMILY EMPLOYEES

One way to provide development opportunities to your family members is to bring them into the business and give them hands-on experience. That brings a plethora of challenges for the founder, the adult child, and the other employees. For teens and young adults, summer employment or part-time work at the ground level enriches your child's life experience and grounds them. For adults who have "launched," they should start in a position that's commensurate with their education, experience, and skills. Best practices recommend that family employees need to be accountable to a supervisor who is not a family member, with appropriate evaluations and feedback.

There need to be clear and consistent guidelines for family participation in the business. Will they start at the bottom? Who will hold them accountable? What requirements must they meet in order to advance? For example, in order to move from summer work to a full-time career track, they might need to complete a college degree or a trade certification. Perhaps they need to apply with a résumé and be interviewed by Human Resources, like any other employee. Those guidelines should be documented in a Family Business Rulebook (also known as a family governance document), and we'll address the specifics of creating a rulebook in the next section.

The second, third, and subsequent generations need to understand that a good career requires diligence, care, education, respect, humility, commitment, and most importantly, desire—the desire to try, fail, learn, and try again. Nurturing a business (or a successor) is like growing a garden—you can't just smell the roses, you have to make a plan, pull some weeds, fertilize, get your hands dirty, and work up a sweat.

Whatever expectations you set should be consistent and transparent. That's especially true in the ways your family members relate to non-family employees. The second or third generation in a family enterprise comes under tremendous pressure because the other employees look at them differently. A lack of clarity about roles, responsibilities, and expectations can create all kinds of miscommunication and misunderstandings that damage family relationships and business morale.

FAMILY SHAREHOLDERS

The second path to consider is for children who are shareholders in the business but not employees. They have an ownership stake, but because they aren't actively participating, they haven't contributed directly to its ongoing success. They don't have the knowledge or the authority to make decisions about the business's operations.

Sometimes these roles become disconnected from each other or come into conflict. For example, one sibling might help manage the business and earn $150,000 a year, while another is a shareholder who doesn't work in the business at all. One year the managing sibling makes a strategic decision that it's in the company's long-term best interest to reinvest the profits rather than pay dividends. The other sibling, who isn't privy to those decisions, might have been counting on that dividend check for an important need in their own life. Now the shareholders are unhappy with the management, and the siblings have conflict with each other, because one of them has an income from the business and the other doesn't.

To avoid major conflicts in business governance, or navigate those that arise, you need a well-planned, clearly documented, and thoroughly communicated set of family business rules.

FAMILY BUSINESS RULEBOOK

Have you ever played a game without rules? Did you win? Was it fun?

How about the people you were playing with? If they didn't know the rules, did they enjoy the experience? Probably not.

Whether football, soccer, hockey, or anything else, you must have clear rules in order to succeed. The same is true in business: healthy family businesses require clear governing documents. Every family member must understand which "circle" they belong to. You need a playbook that lays out when to distribute profits, who gets to make those decisions, and why. It must be reviewed and updated regularly as new family members join the business.

These rules may include topics like:

- The values, mission, and purpose of the family business;
- Entering employment—how to request, qualify for, and be placed in a position;
- Financial disclosures;
- Compensation;
- Performance reviews;
- Personal relationships with coworkers;
- Decision-making and conflict resolution;
- Termination of employment;
- Ownership eligibility;
- Privacy and confidentiality;
- Retirement;
- Dividends and dividend distribution;
- A family council;
- Shareholder agreement requirements, marriage contracts, and other topics that relate to the ownership and transfer of shares.

An important aspect of this rulebook is to build on-ramps for adult children who may decide to join the business later in life. It's normal for young people to have ambitions outside the family business and want to establish an independent career. Later on, they may want to bring those talents and skills back into the family enterprise, and it can be very healthy and helpful to do so. The rulebook should also provide for amicable off-ramps in case a family member chooses to pursue another opportunity.

The whole concept of stewardship and family business succession is for your children to find a role that contributes to the ongoing growth and success of family enterprise. So any role they might fill should meet a real need in the business. The rulebook should outline a clear process for interviewing, supervision, and advancement. It should also define the basic responsibilities and expectations of family members.

The Family Business Rules set out the principles that family members need to follow. It is a living document that evolves with time, and can avert many types of family conflicts, misunderstandings, and potential disasters. When expectations aren't clearly defined in concrete rules from the beginning, unintentional seeds of conflict and misunderstandings begin to germinate. One sibling may believe they have authority over another, or siblings may have competing interests and claims that were never directly stated. I always have at least a few clients in my roster who are navigating tensions or open hostility among their children who work in the family business. If they fail to address them effectively, it invariably means the business will not survive the next generation. Worse, the bonds that hold the family together become unraveled and are difficult to repair.

That's not to say that conflict should be avoided at all costs, though. Conflict in any family business is healthy, as long as there is a mechanism for dealing with conflict constructively. Conflict is life, and out of the resolution of inevitable conflict we become stronger and wiser people. You wouldn't be successful in business if you were completely conflict-avoidant, and you must bring the same courage and skills to dealing with inevitable conflicts within your family. The clarity and structure of a family business rulebook reduces misunderstandings and *destructive* conflict and provides a framework for resolving differences without escalating them into animosity or lasting resentment.

MENTORSHIP

Businesses grow by developing leaders. As you identify talent within your management team and delegate responsibility, you can leverage the skills of those new leaders to accomplish more than you could do on your own. Your children need the same type of opportunities to develop their leadership skills, too. However, successfully mentoring your children is often best accomplished by someone other than you. A parent's job is to teach your children values and provide them with the appropriate life skills that will assist them in securing their future. For their career path and leadership skills, I urge you to bring in a third party—or several different third parties—to coach and mentor them.

First, there's an inherent conflict in roles that many parents have a hard time navigating. As a parent, you have a relationship with your child based on love and encouragement. As a boss or business mentor, that relationship is based on performance and accountability. I have seldom seen a family business that was able to balance those relationships successfully without an outside party to refer to. Either the business suffers from a lack of accountability, or the parent-child relationship suffers from a lack of acceptance and encouragement. Having a different person mentor the next generation shows that you support their growth, while also giving them objective standards and challenges to meet.

Second, your children and grandchildren will most likely require skills that you don't have. The world and the marketplace are constantly evolving, and your business must change to meet those needs and take advantage of those opportunities. The skills that you built in growing your business are not going to carry it forward twenty or thirty years. Your G2 and G3 leaders need to advance beyond you in order to stay competitive.

You might find good mentors for your children in your business partners, senior staff, professional advisors, or a close family friend. Choose someone who demonstrates strong values, is trustworthy, understands your business, and can be relied on to coach them effectively. Ideally, as your children journey through their career path and develop confidence and maturity, they will take responsibility for their personal development and seek out mentors of their own. Encourage them to do so. Becoming proactive in their own growth shows that they're on the right track.

> Businesses grow and prosper
> by developing leaders.

TROUBLESHOOTING TRANSITIONS

Many entrepreneurs are uncomfortable with transition planning because business transition or succession planning means a transfer of control. After all, isn't that why they started a business—so nobody else would tell them what to do? They also worry about whether someone else will be able to ensure business continuity and profitability, since a significant part of their wealth may be wrapped up in the business. Diversifying assets and investments outside an operating business can balance out a business owner's portfolio, increase financial independence, and provide peace of mind about making a business transition.

It's often difficult for entrepreneurs to delegate, and even harder to contemplate turning over the reins entirely. There is so much of themselves in the business that it's hard to let go. That business sat at the breakfast and dinner table just like another child. It went on the family vacations when Dad had to take a call. Nobody just turns their back on a child after raising them for fifteen, twenty or twenty-five years.

It's healthy to acknowledge the worry and responsibility of business ownership and look at it clearly. It runs deeper than most people realize. The truth is, change is inevitable and we don't have total control over our health or the end of our lives. At some point, that business will transition, whether you planned for it or not. The only way to ensure a wise, smooth transition is to plan it intentionally and make the change gradual before you're forced to do so.

CHANGING PERSONAL PRIORITIES

Imagine that your enterprise is a bus, and you're driving it on a long road trip. You can only go so long before you get exhausted. Wouldn't it be nice to know that you had another driver who could swap in for you? It would certainly be safer for that bus and everyone on it if there were another driver who could take over before the original driver started falling asleep at the wheel (assuming they are trained and qualified beforehand). Swapping drivers will also allow that bus to keep moving forward instead of sitting idle whenever you need a rest.

As we age, our willingness and ability to deal with complicated situations changes; this is sometimes called our "threshold of complexity." When we're young, we can juggle so many moving parts, like multitasking on a grand scale. We're growing our families, developing our businesses, meeting the accountant, the lawyer, the insurance specialist, and the financial advisor, meeting new clients, buying and selling companies and buildings, and managing multiple interests within our family enterprise.

Over time, our tolerance for hassle—our threshold of complexity—decreases. The concept of elegant simplicity becomes more attractive. You're willing to pay a little more to simplify your life.

It's much the same as your physical agility. When you're young, you might play sports and do a lot of demanding activities. Over time, you might get a knee injury or wrench your back. You can't ski anymore, so you cycle instead. You don't play tennis, so you switch to golf. You know your limits and modify your plans to suit your needs.

The same holds true for complexity in the day-to-day management of your business enterprise. Sometime around age sixty, if not before, we start to get fed up with all the hassle: staffing issues, financial hiccups, changes in tax legislation, creating new entities, and winding up old ones. You look at all your trusts and holding companies, and think, *I don't even know where to start. Can I just have one afternoon to go fishing?*

The purpose of transitioning is to lighten your load. You spent so many years nurturing your business, and now it's time to start harvesting and pruning. You're driven by your desire to see how far you can go with your success. At some point your priorities may change, and you may want to take more time to enjoy the fruits of your labor.

CHANGING BUSINESS PRIORITIES

I have a group of clients who have been business partners for decades. Between the three of them, they have eight children, most of whom work in the business. The members of the second generation are in their forties now, and there's a great deal of pressure on the business to grow so they can keep supporting their growing families. After all, as one of the sons put it, that business initially started out supporting three families, and now it's supporting seven (plus one hundred employees). Because of this, the business is required to multiply their revenue six to ten times and choose leaders among that second generation who can take the company where it needs to go. After all, they can't have seven presidents, so some difficult decisions need to be made.

Changes in the business environment need to be taken into account. The way that a founder built up their business may not be the best course to help that business flourish in the long term. The business may need to pivot to stay on a trajectory of success. Life is changing, technology advances, industries are evolving at an incredible pace, and the second or third generation of leaders in a company will probably have to make major changes and develop additional strategies in order to continue to grow and remain profitable. That's why it's so important to choose leaders wisely, invest in their development, and plan the transition carefully.

Once upon a time, the state of the economy was measured by how many buggy whips were produced each year. Somewhere, someone is still making buggy whips, I'm sure. But they're a specialty craft item, not a major industry. Now we use new housing starts as a measure of economic growth, but even that is subject to change. The size and type of houses that the market demands are changing, and the real estate market itself has gone through such turmoil in the last few years, who knows how long it will continue to be a reliable indicator of the overall economy? Your business must adapt to inflation, geopolitical factors, and the changing economy in order to stay relevant, stay profitable, and keep growing.

PREPARING FOR A HANDOFF

Your potential successors need to share your values, your drive, your commitment to your business, and understand stewardship. That doesn't mean they need to be a carbon copy of you! They might have complementary skills and perspectives, rather than identical ones. Maybe they'll be smarter than you. Maybe they'll have different ideas about new directions for the business. Those are all good things. The essential element is that they are in it for the same reasons you are. They share your *why*.

In a relay race, one runner passes the baton to the next. This handoff point is crucial, and many races are won or lost by how well the team executes a handoff. If the second runner were standing still, and the first runner had to stop to pass off that baton, the whole team would lose momentum and fall behind. Instead, the two runners pace each other until their strides are matched and their arms are swinging in perfect synchronization.

It's also necessary for the first runner to keep hold of the baton until the second runner has a solid grip, but if they hold on too long, they will knock the second runner off their stride. They must let go at the right moment—not too soon, and not too late. Then the handoff can flow smoothly, and the whole team is set up to win.

> It takes courage and confidence to let go.

As you transition your business or your wealth, plan to work alongside your successor so they can learn from you, and you can help them develop the necessary skills to manage. That will allow you to hone the plan so that the transition becomes seamless. It will also help you see the right time to let go, because you will build trust and confidence that they are fully prepared. Then you can step back and transition yourself into a mentorship role. Your successor, whether a family member or not, will continue to need your wisdom and experience as a resource.

As you give them more and more autonomy, they may make mistakes, but they will learn from them the same way you learned from your own mistakes. After all, your mistakes shaped your skills, your character, and the enterprise you have today. Your successors will grow the same way. Mistakes and failures are natural parts of learning and growing. They're nothing to be afraid of.

A TEAM EFFORT

Only you can instill your personal values and principles about handling money into your children. That's an intimate and powerful part of the parent-child relationship. However, creating family business plans and governance structures are not DIY projects.

You need a team of professional advisors who can pull together the details of these plans, make sure they are practical and consistent, and follow through to ensure you execute them correctly. You probably already have an accountant, a lawyer, and perhaps even a financial planner to help you, but are they prepared for the kind of in-depth planning you really need? Do they have the credentials of a Family Enterprise Advisor (FEA) and the experience to provide a deeper and broader perspective to help you achieve your dreams for your family?

Up to now, we've focused on personal contemplation and family relationships. In the second half of this book, we'll examine the practical, structural side of disaster-proofing your legacy. That will require you to call on professional advisors who can provide you with sound ideas and set those structures up correctly. In order to do that, your team will need to go beyond standardized service packages and work together to customize your plans. In the next chapter, we'll focus on building the team you need.

✎ HOMEWORK

- Do you have a list or snapshot of the whole scope of your family business enterprise? How about your net worth? If not, it's time to create one.
- Does your family understand the scope of your wealth and their future prospects (in general terms, if not in detail)?
- What guiding principles have led you to take the opportunities you chose?
- How does the current structure of your enterprise express your priorities and values?
- Do your children understand and share those priorities?
- What kind of money lessons have you given your children? Are they similar or different from the lessons you grew up with?
- How do you practice transparency and equity in giving to your children?
- Do you need to reset boundaries and expectations with your family about money? How can you help them make that transition?
- What expectations do your children have about owning or working in the family business? Do they match up with your expectations?
- Do you have a family business rulebook? If so, is it up to date? Is it available to consult regularly, or tucked away in some bottom left-hand drawer? Are you respecting the rules?

- Who can you identify as a potential mentor for your children in your personal or professional network?
- What do you actually do all day as the business owner? Whether you're buying, negotiating, managing, rainmaking, or whatever key activities keep your business profitable—those are the activities, contacts, and plans that you need to document and teach to someone else.
- Make a specific goal to teach at least one new skill every six months. After your mentee learns it, they will take over that responsibility.

WISE WORDS

"The hopes of the well-instructed are better than the wealth of the ignorant."

—*Epictetus*

STRATEGIC ACTION PLAN

Objective:

Due Date:

Why is it important?

What will be the end result?

Who will be responsible for this project?

Who to contact:

Deadline:

Thoughts/Notes:

CHAPTER FIVE

PICK YOUR ADVISORY TEAM

Your professional advisors need to collaborate, not just cooperate.

The client wasn't comfortable. The boardroom chairs in his tax lawyer's office looked ergonomic, but something was hitting him wrong. He squirmed.

The lawyer had constructed a very sound and effective plan for dealing with the client's $75 million estate. The goal was to minimize estate tax, and the strategy was "divide and defer." Upon the client's death, his fortune would be put into a spousal trust. His wife would be able to live very comfortably for the rest of her life on the income, and when she died, the capital would go to the client's four children.

As he listened, the client looked at his wife, and around the table at his lawyer, his accountant, and his financial advisor. The accountant and the lawyer gave each other a nod. They'd spent years trying to get this guy's estate documents in place. The purpose of this whole meeting was to hopefully, finally, get that accomplished.

The client picked up the trust papers and put them back down again. He was in the hot seat, all right, but maybe the chair wasn't the problem. He squirmed again.

After all, it was a good plan! The spousal trust was a standard setup. The client looked at his wife again. How could he get his advisors to understand this wasn't a standard situation? This was his second marriage, and the children from his first marriage didn't necessarily get along with wife number two. Everyone was prickly, and there were years of simmering tension. What would it do to his family if his children were frozen out of their inheritance for years or decades until his wife died?

He didn't really care about saving every possible penny in taxes. He had more than enough to provide for his wife, his children, and the tax man. He'd thrown himself into his business (and missed a lot of his children's childhood) to create an ongoing legacy for generations. He'd done a lot of work to rebuild his relationships with his children after a messy divorce from their mother. Wouldn't this plan just blow up everything he'd worked for?

But it's not as if he could say all that out loud, in front of these people, in a business meeting, of all things. Everyone was expecting him to sign. Maybe he'd get an important phone call and have to leave. Maybe he could fake one. He felt a bead of sweat on his upper lip.

All his advisors knew was that they'd finally cornered their recalcitrant client and had a decent shot at finishing this project. He needed an estate plan, for his own good. They needed to close these files and get paid. They could see his discomfort, but they didn't understand it. They had no idea about the underlying conflicts in his family.

They never asked.

A good plan isn't always the right plan.

This client wasn't procrastinating because he was reluctant to put in the time, or because he didn't care. He cared very much about his family and wanted to protect and provide for them. But he knew in his gut that this plan wouldn't meet his personal goals or his family legacy goals. He didn't know how to articulate the emotional and relational issues at play, so he kept shying away from the whole topic.

This kind of resistance indicates a communication breakdown between a wealth holder and his advisors. He wasn't clear on how to express his concerns because the other advisors didn't take the time to ask the real questions—personal, feelings-oriented questions like, "What's keeping you awake at night?" "How do you feel about your family relationships? Are there any relationship issues we should consider in creating your financial and estate plans?"

Estate planning can be very complex. Perhaps the lawyer or accountant who drew up your tax strategy or planned your family trust hasn't distilled it down into layman's terms, and you don't feel confident signing it. Perhaps you have a nagging suspicion that this plan may trigger a family nuclear explosion, but you aren't prepared to admit that to your advisors—or to yourself.

You need advisors who can create a truly customized plan for you and see it through to conclusion. In order to do that, you must assemble a team of discerning, committed professionals who can listen empathetically and collaborate on a comprehensive, interconnected solution. They need to be curious, alert, resourceful and responsive. That team also needs a strong coach who can keep the whole project moving forward and hold everyone—including you—accountable for the results. That way you and your team can create a plan that's a perfect fit for your situation, your goals, your values—your family. A plan like that doesn't come from having the right answers, but from asking deep questions that provoke deep thought.

EMPATHY IS PRICELESS

Most professional advisors like accountants and lawyers have good answers. Come to think of it, they have great answers. They have incredible knowledge as it pertains to tax efficiency, planning, and structures to ensure that there is minimal tax leakage to what has been built. The problem is, they usually focus on questions directly related to their field of expertise. This leaves blind spots in your estate plan.

They just don't always ask enough questions. The most important ones are, "How do you feel about what you have built?" and "Tell me your story."

Professional service providers have a product to sell: their advice and the results that they bring for you. The question you should be asking is whether they are providing a **transaction** or a **process**. A tax structure, a tax return, a will, or an insurance policy are transactions. A process for ensuring that each component of your plan is integrated and harmonized with your vision, your values, and your goals creates **transformation**. The choice is yours: product or process? Transaction or transformation?

Recently a client called to ask for my advice. He'd just received an offer on a commercial property that he hadn't previously thought of selling. It was a lot of money, and he was considering it, but he wasn't sure what to do. I asked him three questions:

- What's the purpose of the building?

    He said that it was for his business, so it could continue to grow and prosper.

- Why is future growth of his family enterprise important to him?

> *He answered that it was important for his retirement, and as a legacy for his family.*

- Then I asked about the net sale proceeds after the taxes were paid and price after taxes. If the sale would impact the growth of his business, would the revenue from the sale fund his retirement and his family legacy?

  He answered no. It wasn't enough.

So, did he want to sell that building? Hell, no.

An empathetic, collaborative advisor is a sounding board. I didn't tell him what to do. I approached his situation with curiosity and kept asking questions until he achieved clarity about what he wanted to do.

More often than not, accountants and lawyers tend to overlook the emotional and relational aspects of financial planning. I'm not sure why this happens. Perhaps it's because during their apprenticeship, they are not trained to ask soft, feely questions; they're on the clock for billable hours, and empathetic exploration is time-consuming. Sometimes they have their own set of taboos around money discussions and may feel that asking personal questions is too "nosy." More often than not, accountants and lawyers aren't trained to address the "mushy stuff," and it's not a natural fit for their temperament. After all, they chose their fields for a reason—they like rules and numbers and everything clearly stated in black and white.

Families aren't black and white. The truth is, they're messy, mushy, and frankly, wonderful! There are emotions, history, differing viewpoints, unstated expectations, and complex dynamics. There are gray areas—big gray areas. Everything is meaningful, but it isn't always logical. An advisor who can't or won't delve into the emotional chasms of family dynamics is robbing their clients of useful advice, because the clients can't know what they don't know.

Estate planning always carries an emotional burden, whether it's spoken or not. Facing our own mortality can be overwhelming. All kinds of thoughts race through our minds—dark thoughts, foolish thoughts, funny thoughts, angry thoughts, frightened thoughts. Life and death are two sides of a coin. They can't be separated because both sides make a whole. It can be very difficult to think clearly when it's time to plan for your own death. You need to know that your advisory team has more than the necessary skills to ensure a tax efficient estate plan. Often, we believe that every family shares common themes and concerns, because we're all human. At the same time, each family is enriched by different personalities, unique individuals, unique experiences, and a very personal family story. In order for advisors to be effective, they need to be curious and alert to dig deep into those unique aspects and understand them. They require a sense of resourcefulness to help deal with the issues that are not in their lane of expertise. They also need the humility to admit when they don't have all the answers, and the willingness to connect a client to someone who does. This is what good, collaborative advice is all about.

DIG DEEP

Deep discovery involves everything we've been discussing throughout this book: your personal history and how it affects your beliefs and attitudes about family and money. The way we grow up usually defines our drive (or lack thereof), our decision-making, how we manage our wealth, and our unconscious behavior around work, money, and family. Just like the process you went through in the first four chapters, the process of deep discovery helps lift the fog so you can see clearly how your intentions for your family and your wealth fit together with all the moving parts of corporate structures and legal documents. Deep discovery also helps uncover any areas where some of your decisions may be misaligned and need adjusting to better fit your preferences, attitudes, and values.

Discovery questions include reflecting on your past, such as how often you heard your parents talk about money, and in what context. Did both parents work outside the home, or was it more traditional? Did you know how much your parents earned? Did you see the choices they made about managing their finances? Did they clip coupons and shop sales? Did they spend frivolously or were they very frugal? Were they intentional about planning for the future? Were they generous? To whom? Looking back, do you think their patterns were healthy and reasonable in their circumstances? How has this impacted your relationship to the wealth that you have created? What did you think about your family's money situation when you were growing up? Did you think you were poor, rich, or somewhere in between? Perhaps the thought never crossed your mind.

The way your parents talked to you about your own prospects and your future may have been another important factor in shaping your actions and choices. If your father told you that you'd never amount to anything, you might be driven to succeed in order to prove him wrong—maybe even so driven that you have trouble knowing when to stop and take a rest or knowing when you've built enough and it's time to enjoy it. Or maybe your parents insisted on you having an education because they did not have that opportunity growing up. These conversations may have been the catalyst to your success.

An advisor who is curious and takes the time to genuinely listen to your history and uncover your deepest thoughts, concerns, and values can use those same skills to collaborate with other members of your advisory team. Just as deep discovery is about more than taking down data, collaboration among your advisors is a next-level process.

COLLABORATION, NOT JUST COOPERATION

Your professional advisors—legal, accounting, and financial—understand that they need to *cooperate* with each other to serve their client: I'll be nice to you, and you'll be nice to me. We aren't working on the same thing or building anything together, but we'll pass over information upon request, not waste each other's valuable time, and be generally helpful about practical matters. Each person stays in their own lane and treats the others with respect.

That's all well and good, but it's really just a minimum standard of professional courtesy. You can and should expect more.

Collaboration goes a lot deeper. It means that everyone is helping to build the same house. Your advisors proactively share information that could impact each other's advice. They understand your goals as a joint project, and brainstorm together about the best way to meet those goals and fulfill your values. They share their concerns as it pertains to personal information that may impact various planning strategies and recommend adjustments to ensure that "best in class" solutions are being presented. Collaboration requires your advisors to listen to each other more than they talk. They share in-depth knowledge about your financial situation, your family dynamics, and your mindset.

When your advisors collaborate, you won't always be there in the room steering the conversation. But that's to your benefit, because they can brainstorm all kinds of new ideas before they present them to you. Collaboration can be messy, but the end result can be wonderful. The biggest challenges to collaboration are silos, lingo, and ego.

BEWARE OF SILOS

Each profession—accounting, law, insurance, and so forth—comes with a particular lens through which an advisor will see your situation. These unconscious biases can give your advisors tunnel vision, so that they only see one approach to your planning, rather than seeing the whole picture of the way your plans will affect you and your family's financial future. They will give advice about your planning based on their own perspective, and sometimes that will result in conflicting advice, or blind spots where your plan doesn't address your deepest concerns and needs. It's like that old saying: "When all you have is a hammer, everything looks like a nail."

In general, tax accountants focus on the Three Ds to address every business tax situation: deduct, divide, and defer. Insurance advisors focus on risk, so they see three different Ds: death, disability, and disease (referring to critical illness coverage). Lawyers have Three Ls: litigation, liability, and loss.

A hammer-and-nail approach can have serious unintended consequences. For example, let's look at "deduct, divide, and defer." You deduct as many things as you can, according to what's permissible under the tax law. Deferring taxes means postponing them to the future so that you can take advantage of compound interest and growth in the value of your assets, whereas paying taxes today could impede that growth. Dividing refers to splitting income and assets into different "buckets" for different tax treatment, such as tax advantaged giving or placing assets into a trust.

How do these impact your family dynamics? Well, if you simply focus on deferring your taxes, you could really be deferring important conversations with your family about legacy, values, your goals, or how to teach your children the necessary skills to manage wealth and ensure their well-being. If you focus solely on dividing your assets to save taxes, you may end up dividing your family members because of misunderstandings. If you focus only on deducting every possible penny, you could wind up deducting a family member from your plans by leaving them out of important discussions and decisions that they care about and want to be part of. You wind up with a whole other set of Three Ds: disconnection, disillusionment, and disaster.

Sometimes clients deliberately keep their advisors siloed from one another, thinking that it will save them from paying higher fees. They will give partial information and request one aspect of their planning from their accountant, another from their lawyer, another from their financial advisor, and so forth. They believe they can orchestrate the grand plan on their own, with the professionals crafting disparate pieces of the puzzle. Let me tell you right now—that never works out well in the long run. One of two things usually happens in that scenario. Either the client winds up with conflicting documents that need to be revised later, or they get overwhelmed with the complexity of all these moving parts and never execute anything. Unfinished and conflicting plans create messes. Messes require lawyers to clean them up. Soon, you find yourself in a self-perpetuating cycle of lawyers, upon lawyers, upon lawyers, accountants, advisors, and fees upon fees to clean up the mess.

Ninety-nine percent of shareholder agreements, wills, and other planning documents have major deficiencies due to a lack of collaboration among advisors. A collaborative team shares their different perspectives in order to find the most appropriate strategy for you. One may look at things from a risk standpoint, and another from an investment standpoint, a legal perspective, or a tax perspective. By sharing these views, they can expand their peripheral vision and work toward solutions that result in a more comprehensive and customized plan.

BEWARE OF LINGO

Sometimes a client will have a complete set of plans and legal documents, but never execute them. That's usually because they are written in professional jargon or "legalese," and the professionals who drew them up didn't take the time to explain in simple language how important they are, what they mean, and how they achieve the intended result.

Each sentence and nuance is significant. Whether a clause says "and" or "or" can make a tremendous difference in the outcome. Using "but" rather than "if" radically alters the impact. A layperson would need four different dictionaries just to understand the legal boilerplate.

So instead of signing these important and necessary documents, business owners do nothing. I can't tell you how many legal documents end up in the bottom left-hand drawer of a desk, unsigned. They're never seen again until there is a disagreement, a divorce, or an emergency. By then it's too late.

Unfortunately, the majority of professional advisors are paid for their time, not for results. They will leave these final, crucial steps incomplete, because they aren't getting paid to chase after their clients. The number of shareholder agreements without signatures, marriage contracts started and never implemented, draft wills left unsigned, is staggering. This procrastination leads to broken families and resounding disasters. It's all totally unnecessary. A collaborative team that listens and communicates should also ensure that you understand what you're signing, how it works, and why.

BEWARE OF EGO

As powerful as it is to avoid costly mistakes, collaboration isn't always easy. It requires each person to put their ego, ever so gently, in their back pocket. They must share information, but also context and insight about their client that goes beyond data—like the risks and opportunities inherent in the client's primary goals. It only works if everyone involved has the desire to understand each other's point of view and commits to keeping an open mind, so they can design the right solution for the client. Each professional on your advisory team must be open to learning, or to having their misconceptions corrected. They have to put the client's interests above their own desire to be the smartest person in the room.

That goes against the grain for some people because you don't get to be successful without having confidence in your own abilities. Trusting other people's abilities requires a whole different level of confidence. When your advisors are merely cooperating, they may inadvertently wind up in a battle of egos, with each of them wanting to preserve their position of influence.

I'll be the first to admit that there are things I don't understand. For example, here in Canada there's a tax provision under Section

84.1. I've had it explained to me countless times and every so often, I forget about the nuances of this important tax provision and need to be reminded of the impact in a client's planning. Whenever I want to help a client plan for their taxes, the tax lawyer or accountant will remind me about this flipping Section 84.1, and I have to have it explained all over again so I can design a more effective solution.

That interaction isn't adversarial. I brainstorm a strategy, and another team member brings up our constraints. I rely on that professional's expertise to ensure that I don't screw up and give inappropriate advice. We're working together to stretch each other's thinking beyond our own narrow focus. In the end, we (not I) come up with a solution that respects the various tax and legal constraints and offers the client the control and freedom to achieve the tax, legacy, and financial goals that they set out from the beginning.

Ultimately, collaboration is rare because it's hard work! Many advisors prefer to stick with tried-and-true standard structures because it saves time and money. It can also save the hassle of challenging a client who thinks they already know exactly what they want. Some advisors are happy to take orders and fill in the blanks. A collaborative team can dig deeper and offer alternatives that a busy entrepreneur who is managing their business might not even know to ask about.

That's exactly what happened to the uncomfortable client in our story. I happened to know the backstory about his family situation, because I'd worked with them for years. I called a time-out on the meeting and took the other advisors out to lunch to fill them in. As a result, the attorney scrapped his plug-and-play spousal trust and offered up a whole new way to set up the estate. The client secured some additional life insurance to provide liquidity to pay the estate tax and achieved his goal of leaving a legacy for his children and his spouse in a simple, clear fashion. (Kind of like the way he ran all his various businesses—simple and clear.) The revised recommendation resonated with the clients' overall family legacy goals, so he was finally able to say "yes" and execute those documents. When your advisors are prepared to collaborate on a customized plan for you, they become a strong team that can help achieve your true long-term goals. Most importantly, this ensures that you, the wealth creator, continue to be in the driver's seat and lead the plan, instead of being led into a potential labyrinth of complexity and confusion.

THE TEN DOMAINS OF FAMILY WEALTH

The Ten Domains is a framework for thinking about family wealth developed by the Ultra-High Net Worth Institute.[1] Ultra-high net worth is usually defined as having over $30 million USD in liquid assets, but these same areas of concern apply to family enterprises whether you meet that threshold or not. This is a very useful model for thinking about your wealth planning because it gives equal weight to all the different aspects of your family's life and work.

There are three main components: human advancement, wealth creation and stewardship, and the cultivation of family capital. Human advancement addresses supporting and developing family members to be the best that they can be. That includes health and well-being, family dynamics, and social impact or philanthropy. Whatever personal aspirations your children and grandchildren may have to live a good life and make the world a better place, these domains all address their growth as human beings.

---

[1] "The Ten Domains of Family Wealth," The UHNW Institute, 2022, https://www.uhnwinstitute.org/resource-library.

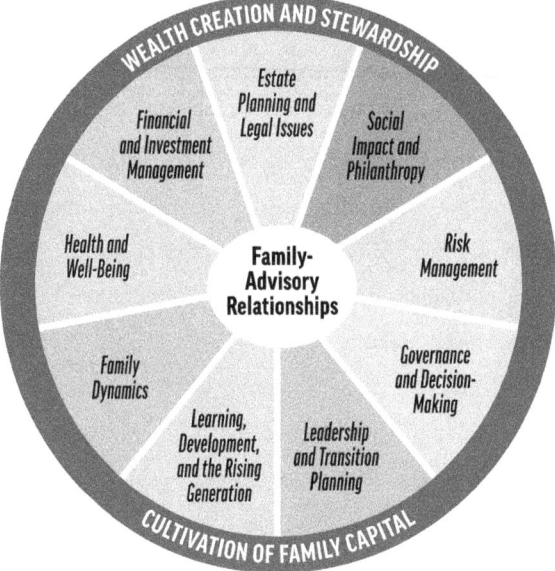

Copyright 2022 UHNW Institute. Used by permission.

Wealth creation and stewardship integrate your tax and legal considerations with risk management in a cohesive way, so that they're harmonized with the goals and values of the wealth holder and their family. This area addresses everything to do with growing, protecting, and preserving your financial legacy.

The third area is the cultivation of family capital. That encompasses everything to do with your family's participation in the business and handling wealth, including financial literacy, leadership and mentorship, transition planning, and family business governance.

I'm addressing all these domains in this book, albeit in a slightly different way. The point I want to draw your attention to is the center of the wheel: the client-advisor relationship. This relationship touches all the other domains. Your advisory team needs to understand and appreciate all the different domains of family wealth and the complex ways that they interact. That way, they can ensure that their recommendations address your values, concerns, and hopes as it relates to the overall well-being of your family and wealth.

I'd like to point out a few key concepts that this diagram illustrates particularly well. First, all the slices of this pie are the same size. One area is not larger or more important than another. Now, at certain points in your life, one area may be more urgent or more complicated than another. There's a natural ebb and flow of life that will dictate which domains need more attention at any given time. Overall, however, they are all of equal significance. Your advisory team needs a holistic, unified approach to harmonize all these domains without giving any of them short shrift.

Next, since all the slices of the pie intersect in the middle, they all touch each other and affect each other. If you think about it, you'll see how this is true in real life. If you're extremely stressed and not at your best mentally, that impacts how well you can make decisions. If you aren't well physically, that impacts your ability to get insurance, which is an important element of risk management and estate preservation. If the family dynamics between your children are contentious, that could impact your legal planning for your estate, your transition planning for your business, and potentially your own health and well-being. Everything is connected.

Your advisors don't all need to be specialists in every area, but I encourage you to look for people who are curious and thoughtful about all these different aspects. They need to be flexible, resourceful, and have discernment about the different ways their recommendations may affect all the slices of your personal pie.

> Managing, growing, and protecting your wealth
> requires time, effort, and people.

WHO BELONGS ON YOUR TEAM?

The first team member you need is, of course, an accountant. You want to work with a firm that can do more than prepare individual and corporate tax returns. You want someone who can ask questions, think deeply about your overall financial picture, and help you achieve your goals. However, every problem isn't a tax problem. You want to work with an accountant who is willing to take a broader view and doesn't want everything to be a nail just because they have a hammer.

You also need a lawyer to help you draw up business and estate plan documents. Generally, lawyers are trained and have the mindset to avoid litigation and consider the worst-case scenario for everything. You need a cool and cautious head on your team, but again—look for someone who isn't so focused on their own viewpoint that they lose sight of the bigger picture.

When it comes to finding the right attorney, experience counts. A friend of mine who is a lawyer once told me that when he's in litigation, if the opposing counsel is in their twenties or thirties, he knows he's in for a fight, because younger lawyers are hungry for a scrap. Those fights usually wind up costing both clients a lot more money. If the lawyer on the other side is in his fifties, they're probably going to sit down and work out a resolution that's far more efficient and fairer for both parties. They don't have anything to prove, and their ego isn't invested in winning. They can take the long view and put their client's best interests first.

Your financial advisor also belongs on your team. Some advisors are investment focused, and some are risk focused. While both specialties are valuable, you need to choose a person who can think creatively about meeting your needs and is curious to ask the right questions about your entire situation (not just about investment planning or insurance strategies). I have seen scenarios where the client is "sold" on a strategy before taking into account the specifics of current tax laws, the client's overall personal situation, and their goals. I have seen simple planning turn into a mess of complexity, and complex situations turn into a mess of taxes, due to lack of appropriate and relevant planning.

One of these team members—and it could be any one of them—needs to have the discernment and commitment to dig deep into the recesses of your heart and mind, to understand your history, your current needs, and your hopes for the future. They need to take the time to understand the complexity of your family's relationships and patterns. That person can become the "coach" of your team.

YOUR FAMILY ADVISOR COACH

I always believed that the quarterback was one of the most valuable players on the team. I was reminded by a very successful (and humble) football player that this is not true. The most valuable person on a successful team is the head coach. It is the coach who builds the team, helps them work together to achieve a common goal, and gently encourages and inspires you to achieve your dreams. The advisor you choose as your coach is responsible for guiding the others toward a personalized plan that will resonate with you, make sense to you, and keep you motivated to finish the project. Also, someone who is accountable to a deadline to get things done!

If you don't have a coach, things get stalled and you get stuck. You need someone to keep moving the ball so that all the team members keep making progress. Let's face it, if you are a business owner, you are busy—very busy.

> More often than not, one of the professionals on your team will offer to take the lead and become the coach. If not, ask one of them to step up. You can identify which team member would make a great coach by the following attributes:
>
> 1. Curiosity;
> 2. Resourcefulness;
> 3. Alertness;
> 4. Responsiveness;
> 5. Consistency in following up to get things done.

Your coach needs to gather information from you about your family structure, your business structure, financials, family relationships and any worries or concerns that are keeping you awake at night. It is key that they share their insight with the advisory team. They might need to follow up with the lawyer or the accountant to make sure they have all the information they need and are completing their tasks. It could mean chasing you to make sure you're answering questions, keeping scheduled meetings, and signing the appropriate documents.

Your team needs to huddle and confer so they can collaborate and communicate, but if they stay huddled forever, nothing moves. The coach has to hold them accountable to play as a team and keep moving forward. Ultimately, they're in charge of getting the plan executed so there are no loose ends.

You need someone who is sharp and has great expertise in their field. You want someone who is curious about new developments in the law, new approaches to planning, and, especially, someone who's curious and genuinely interested in you. You want someone who is resourceful, responsive, and fully invested in getting you the best possible results. They need to communicate clearly and proactively and set reasonable expectations about their process and timeline for getting things done. They also need to stay in touch with you and answer your questions promptly and fully. They should ask about your communication preferences and present information in a clear, understandable way that is customized to your learning preference.

Entrepreneurs, as a group, tend to be thick-skinned and driven to succeed. (Otherwise they would not be so resilient in the face of adversity.) They require a coach who listens and challenges their thinking when necessary. An advisor needs to have confidence, not arrogance—someone who will listen to you, understand and be empathetic to your priorities, and who won't let you off the hook. Confidence is when you are sure of your own knowledge and abilities. Arrogance is when you want to impress other people and make sure they know how smart and capable you are. Confidence allows you to admit what you don't know.

A COACH LIKE NO OTHER

A healthy and successful team will also need assistant coaches with particular specialties. In Chapter Two, I mentioned family financial therapists, who can help navigate tension or conflict or initiate healthy discussions about money, family, and relationships. This is a growing field of professionals who specialize in addressing family dynamics and intergenerational issues. If your loved ones are uncomfortable discussing the future, lack direction, or have a hard time communicating productively with one another, a family financial therapist or psychologist trained specifically in the area of family business can be a great addition to your advisory team.

There are many misconceptions about therapy, so let's take the word "therapy" and replace it with "coaching." There are many financial and family coaches with psychology degrees that help families gain clarity and confidence in life skills for communication, finance, family, careers, and business. These professionals are especially helpful for family business enterprises, because of the complex relationship issues that can arise. Coaches help us understand ourselves and our attitudes. They can provide direction for younger family members who may feel overwhelmed by the wealth that was created before them and help them find their own purpose. They can also uncover money scripts or unconscious patterns that may hold us back from fully enjoying our families and our wealth.

PERSONAL QUALITIES

We've talked about empathy, curiosity, and collaboration, and those are all facets of the type of advisor to look for. I think the best way to sum up all the qualities you need in an advisor—no matter what their specialty may be—is low self-interest. Excellent advisors are interested in your family, in the other members of the team, and, of course, in you and your needs. They should have genuine concern for your well-being and best interests, and a thoughtful approach to weighing your best interests in what may be a complicated situation.

For example, my advisory practice often recommends life insurance as a solution to ensure tax-free liquidity to pay estate taxes, equalize family bequests, provide funds to buy out shares upon death, and giving to charity. More often than not, I know my clients need insurance. I may estimate or believe that a client needs a specific amount of insurance, but I want to make sure my recommendations are based on what they want and why—not just my own opinion. It's also important that when they come to a decision, they have considered all the factors that matter to them and taken into account all the options they have besides insurance. That way, they have clarity and confidence in their decision, because they understand how it connects with what they want, who they want it for, and why.

I also know that risk mitigation is only one component of their overall estate plan. That's why I value collaboration to find the best tax advisor, the best legal advisor, and so forth. The client needs all of us to think deeper about these plans and documents, how they will affect family harmony and the individual family members.

You need advisors who understand that sometimes their recommendations may create other problems, and who admit their mistakes, quickly and readily. A mistake in a complex enterprise plan is like a dog vomiting behind the couch—the longer you hide it, the harder it is to clean up and the smellier it gets. You have to find it and fix it as soon as possible. The business and tax environment change quickly, and the tax planning landscape is becoming more and more complex for successful family enterprises.

Above all, you want to work with professionals who know their own strengths and blind spots and are willing to ask for help or refer you to others if that's the best thing for you. A lawyer who specializes in estate litigation may not be the best person for family business succession plans or shareholder agreements. An accountant who specializes in how to get research and development tax credits may not be the best at estate planning. That's fine, as long as they can point you to the people who can fill those gaps, instead of doing a mediocre job in order to maintain the client relationship. The best advisors are the ones who say, "I don't know the answer to that, but I can find out." Or "Here's the person who can answer it, and you should talk to them."

CHANGING PLAYERS

From time to time a sports team needs to shake up the roster in order to be more effective. The same is true for your team of advisors. Indeed, sometimes it isn't up to you—advisors move away, retire, or go on to other positions. Your attorney might become a judge and give up their private practice. If your enterprise goes on for many generations, it may outlive them. The advisor you worked with when you started a small business may not have the expertise or the capacity to scale up and deal with the issues you encounter later on. Perhaps you have a longtime advisor who is set in their ways and isn't prepared to work collaboratively.

Some of your advisors may only be needed occasionally or for a short time. For example, if you use a facilitator to lead family meetings, they may be a pinch-hitter rather than a permanent member of your team. If you have a family financial coach or career counselor, they may specialize in certain life stages, like working with teens.

Ultimately, it's about fit. The members of your advisory team need to fit the needs of your family and your business. It's normal for you to cycle members on and off the team. It's like a highway—some people are coming on, some people are exiting, but you're all headed in the same direction: to live out your values and goals for your family's future.

If this seems like a lot of work, you guessed right. After all, a successful family business enterprise was not built in a day! It took time, effort, an occasional failure or two, and persistence to stay the course. Managing, growing, and protecting your wealth requires time, effort, and people.

CONNECT YOUR TEAM TO YOUR FAMILY

In order to truly disaster-proof your family business legacy, your family members need to know your advisory team. When you're gone, they need to know who to call. Beyond that, they need to have a preexisting relationship with these team members, so they can trust and rely on their guidance when required.

You could make these introductions in a family meeting, or ideally as part of the ongoing series of money conversations we discussed in Chapter Two. This may even be a good opportunity to circle back to Chapter One and break your silence by sharing the contents of your will. Don't panic! I understand that, depending on your situation when you started this book, and how quickly you're working through it, you might not be ready to talk about bequests and dollar amounts yet. That's fine. You don't necessarily have to. The important thing is that you discuss the structure of your estate plan, and your reasons for those choices. The deeper your conversations with them about values, history, and family stories, the more likely that your children and grandchildren will be inspired to become good stewards of that wealth. In addition to introducing them to your lawyer, accountant, and so forth, make sure they know who you have chosen as your executor, and why.

My husband and I haven't yet shared the full extent of our assets with our children, but we have told them about the important points of what we have and how it is structured. We explained what an executor does, who our executors are, and who the trustees of our family trust will be. They are generally aware of the scope of our assets, be it real estate, holding corporations, or life insurance. They don't need every detail right now, but they know where to find everything and who to talk to should anything happen to us. We'll talk more about organizing your documents and keeping them accessible in Chapters Eight and Nine.

I own my own business, and my husband owns two, so there's some complexity in our estate plan. We made sure our children know who our accountant and lawyer are, as they will play an important role in settling our estate so that our children are not overwhelmed. When someone dies, particularly an entrepreneur, there are many moving parts. There are also certain actions that need to be taken over a couple of years in order to minimize estate taxes, and we explained the timeframe to our children, so they'll be prepared. Most importantly, we have taken the time to explain the "why."

An excellent way to create a strong connection between your adult children and your advisors is to help them set up their own planning when they become adults. This can range from preparation of income tax returns to having them draw up their own wills and powers of attorney. This experience will enable them to learn about the importance of planning and take ownership of their personal assets and responsibilities. This often provides an opportunity for them to ask questions and learn about *why* it is important to have wills and powers of attorney. This exercise will be the first building block toward financial literacy, opening up a conversation about values, responsibility, and stewardship.

A client of mine learned a lot about his own children when they went through this exercise. I had recommended that their children, ages eighteen and twenty, prepare a will and power of attorney. They had accumulated some personal savings and investments. Their son told them that he thought he should leave everything to his sister, because he felt that his parents already had plenty of money, so his sister might need it more. They were touched because they hadn't realized how protective he felt toward his sister. Their daughter, in turn, decided to leave several thousand dollars to a particular charity and the balance back to the parents, since they had supported her with private school and her university education. They had different perspectives and different outcomes, yet both perspectives showed a deep sense of gratitude, generosity, and reflection. It was a rather pleasant surprise to their parents! Don't put it off. Don't miss out on these opportunities to know your kids better.

> **PURPOSEFUL PLANNING**
>
> The Purposeful Planning Institute (of which I'm a member) is a wonderful resource for wealth holders seeking professionals who can help them create a values-driven estate plan. It was founded by John A. Warnick, a tax attorney and family legal advisor. After a long career in estate law, he felt that his practice, and the industry as a whole, focused on strategies and tactics rather than on vision and intentionality. The Institute brings together family business advisors, lawyers, psychologists, accountants, and financial advisors like me, who want to help clients think deeply and plan creatively for their family's legacy. When you're seeking out collaborative, innovative advisors, look for PPI membership as one of their credentials. Professionals who have the designation FEA (family enterprise advisors) are also trained to navigate the complexities of successful family business enterprises.

INVEST IN FAMILY HARMONY

Let's be realistic—deep discovery and customized planning take time. That time costs money. The reality is that when you actually see a higher invoice from your advisor, you may wonder whether the extra fees are really worth it.

Well, it depends. Are these fees an expense, or an investment? A personalized plan that is tailored to your family's unique situation could potentially save you hundreds of thousands of dollars in litigation fees and tax obligations. Most importantly, it could spare your family irreparable damage from family disputes over money. Someone once told me that strong families create strong businesses, not the other way around.

> **Spending a bit more for collaborative planning will certainly pay off in the long run.**

I can assure you that if you have the right advisory team that takes the time to understand what you want and why, the value you receive in exchange for this investment is so much greater than the cost. You'll get clarity on the scope and impact of what you actually own, as well as your tax obligations and risks. You'll regain control over your wealth, because you will see new options and opportunities that you never thought of. There's a saying that it's a mistake to be penny wise and pound foolish. It's an even bigger mistake to be money wise and people foolish. When it comes to the cost of leaving your family in a mess—the cost of pain, stress, anger, and destruction—you simply can't put a price tag on family harmony and well-being.

Would you buy a luxury car for $90,000 and skip the $5,000 warranty? The same logic applies here. Spending a bit more for the time and expertise involved in collaborative planning will certainly pay off in the long run. The biggest benefit to all of this is that you, the wealth creator, will have clarity and control of what you have worked a lifetime to build. You will be remembered for wisdom instead of negligence. Building wealth is more than a privilege, it is a responsibility.

A collaborative model for customized planning isn't industry standard—yet. It should be, and I believe it soon *will* be. Right now, there are many excellent advisors who aren't yet working this way because their clients aren't asking for it or aren't open to it. When you're interviewing a new member of your professional team of advisors, or when you discuss your planning with your existing advisors, you may need to broach the concept of a collaborative model and set expectations for the way you want the team to collaborate. See if any of them has the courage to step up their game and take on this role. If no one is able to do so, ask them who they might recommend for you to interview, to determine if they are the right fit for your particular family business enterprise.

First, make the introductions. Set up an initial meeting, even if it's just an informal coffee or lunch, and bring your advisors together. Ask their thoughts about planning, their expertise, and how deep of a bench they may have on their own team to draw on other specialties. Ask about their experience in working collaboratively, and if the approach is new to them, how they feel about the idea.

Word of mouth can be useful in finding collaborative advisors. If one of your team members is particularly thoughtful and collaboratively minded, ask them for recommendations. Every good lawyer knows a slew of accountants, and accountants know financial advisors, and vice versa. Once you find an advisor who takes the time to ask interesting questions, listens to you, and understands where you're coming from, they'll have all the information they need to recommend a great fit. There's cross-pollination among professional advisors in all specialties.

Building a collaborative team takes time and effort. It may seem like a lot of hassle and expense, but every minute and dollar are investments in family peace, prosperity and well-being for your family, and an enriching family legacy that will hopefully sustain many generations.

Once you have your team in place, it's time to start making concrete plans. Strategic tax planning is one component, and we'll discuss that next.

HOMEWORK

- Write down the names of your accountant, lawyer, financial advisor, and other members of your advisory team. Do they know each other? If not, introduce them.
- Do your team members collaborate together, or merely cooperate with each other?
- Does your spouse know your advisory team? Do your children? If they don't, it is time to schedule an introductory meeting. In the meantime, if you got hit by a bus tomorrow, would your family know where to find your advisors' phone numbers?
- Are there issues with family dynamics or communication problems that might make it a good idea to consult a family financial therapist?
- Who is your head coach? If you don't have one, could one of your existing advisors take on that role?
- Pick your most likely head coach and call them for a meeting. Tell them you're ready to get your plans in shape. If they can't help you, ask them who you should talk to.

> **WISE WORDS**
>
> "None of us is as smart as all of us."
>
> —*Ken Blanchard, author of* The One Minute Manager

STRATEGIC ACTION PLAN

Objective:

Due Date:

Why is it important?

What will be the end result?

Who will be responsible for this project?

Who to contact:

Deadline:

Thoughts/Notes:

CHAPTER SIX

TAXES: TRUTH OR CONSEQUENCES

*Financial freedom and estate planning are
about more than avoiding taxes.*

K.C. Irving, patriarch of the Irving family of New Brunswick, started out with a small service station in Bouctouche, New Brunswick in the mid-1920s. Soon, he expanded to a Ford automobile franchise in Saint John. Over the years, he built a complex, vertically integrated family enterprise encompassing oil and gas, timberland, building supplies, trucking, steel, shipyards, engineering, and media. Today, Irving Oil operates the largest refinery in Canada and supplies nearly a fifth of US oil imports. The family have some of the most extensive landholdings in the world and are the fifth largest private landowner in America. The family wealth is estimated between $7 billion and $12 billion.

However, the full extent of the family's holdings is anyone's guess. Since their businesses are privately held, information about their value and the family's net worth are closely guarded secrets. What is known is that K.C. Irving had an overriding interest in avoiding business and estate taxes. He wrangled with the Canadian government over tax policy, and eventually placed most of his business interests into a trust in Bermuda, where they were beyond the reach of the Canada Revenue Agency.

In 1971, he left Canada entirely. He established foreign residency in Bermuda and returned to visit New Brunswick every year. To maintain his foreign resident status, his total time in Canada each year was limited to six months, less one day. When he died in 1992, he was buried in Bermuda, rather than at home in New Brunswick. He spent the last twenty years of his life commuting on a forced schedule, without a home of his own in his own hometown. But at least he didn't pay estate tax.

Many business owners—and many tax advisors—view income, business, and estate taxes as a crushing burden to be avoided at any cost. Accountants and lawyers dream up complex schemes (that the client may not even comprehend) to divide and defer every possible penny in taxes.

Tax planning is important, but taxes should not be the driving force of your life or your estate planning decisions. At some point, you have to ask what those tax savings are costing you in time, energy, complexity, professional fees, and wear and tear on your relationships. A balanced approach will serve you and your family's best interests in the long run.

FACE THE TRUTH

I was a kid long before the Internet existed, much less Snapchat and Instagram. When our parents told us to go play, we had two choices. We could go outside in the neighborhood and play on the street with a friend, or we could watch whatever was on television. There were so many goofy comedies, dramas, and soap operas, but it seems like there were a lot more game shows than there are today. One of my favorites was *Truth or Consequences*.

In case you don't remember, it was a trivia game. The contestants were on the clock to answer a question within a couple of seconds. If they answered wrong or ran out of time, they had a consequence, which was some kind of ridiculous stunt. It was hilarious!

I like to use this metaphor to talk to clients about estate planning and taxes. We only have a limited amount of time to get it right, because the clock is ticking on all of us. And if we get it wrong—or delay by indecision and procrastination—there are consequences. While the consequences on *Truth or Consequences* were fun and harmless, the real-life consequences for your family can be serious and permanent. For example, a lack of liquidity in your estate plan may place your family in a position where they are required to sell your best assets at fire-sale prices in order to pay estate taxes. Even worse, if you inadvertently leave family members gifts of disproportionate value, it could result in World War III and the destruction of family relationships.

> Face the truth about your tax obligations,
> or deal with the consequences.

The first step to getting your estate plan on the right track is to begin with the truth: *What* do you have? *Who* do you want to leave it to, and why? Then take an inventory of all that you have. This will include your business(es), personal property, real estate, your investment portfolio, family heirlooms—all the stuff that you own and never really thought about. Attach a value to each item on your list, note in brackets what it cost you, and total everything up.

Present the list to your financial advisor, accountant, and lawyer.

At least one of them will be able to help you calculate your estate tax obligation upon death. The three of them together will be able to provide advice on different ways to create tax efficiencies. As we discussed in Chapter Five, this consultation should include asking questions about your reasons why, values, and goals. These discussions will not only help you choose the best tax planning strategies, they will be the catalyst to share these truths with your family, so that they are not left with surprises that result in anger and confusion.

It's vital that you acknowledge one painful truth about your taxes: they are an inescapable reality of living in a democratic society. In Canada, if you don't pay your taxes, you will be charged interest (and penalties). In the States, you could wind up in jail. (It might take a decade before you're tracked down, but the penalties can be harsh.) It is understandable that people prefer to avoid discussing such uncomfortable topics, partly because there are so many more enjoyable things to do with their time! The cold, hard truth is that there are no guarantees in life except death and taxes. The reality of estate tax obligations won't go away just because you don't want to talk about it. Ignoring the issue actually makes the problem more expensive and often disastrous.

WALK YOUR TALK

The way you approach your estate planning sends a message to your family about your values and demonstrates leadership. I can't tell you the number of times I have heard children of successful entrepreneurs say to me, "I don't understand. Mom and Dad were so amazingly brilliant and successful, why did they not take the time to plan for their taxes? Why did they leave us this mess?"

How does your thinking about tax planning connect to your personal values? I believe every hard-working citizen has the right to organize their financial affairs in the most tax efficient way possible—within the confines of tax laws, of course! However, when these structures begin to erode the foundations of your value system, additional reflection may be required. Don't let the tax tail wag the dog.

Tax is a relativity game.

I have had many conversations with successful business owners about income taxes. I recall a young business owner in his mid-forties, who was earning over a million dollars in income, always started a meeting by harping on how much he was paying in taxes. He complained about his advisors' lack of creativity. I gently reminded him that with advances in technology and constant changes in legislation, his advisors were serving him well in providing effective tax planning within the confines of the law. After all, he didn't want to resort to drug smuggling or money laundering, right?

I asked him, "Would you like a guaranteed, legal way to pay no taxes at all? Nothing?"

Of course, he jumped at it.

I recommended that he take his house, his business, all his retirement savings, his real estate portfolio, and his personal property, and give it away to charity. He'd become homeless, and then the government would take care of him. He might get a room, or he might have to share. He might get a couple of meals a day. But the good news was, he wouldn't have to pay any taxes!

Would you make that choice? Neither would he.

Tax is a relativity game. You have to pay them, relative to how much you make, so keep it in perspective. Paying taxes isn't inherently bad. It means you're making money. If you feel driven to save every penny, beyond what's reasonable, you have to ask why.

Are you focusing on building a legacy for your family, or are you building an army of lawyers and accountants to defend your turf and minimize your tax? Hiring many advisors costs money, too—are you saving more than you spend? Is your team balanced, or a drain on your resources? Does their advice give you a healthy perspective, or cause confusion? Is all this effort really benefiting you in the ways that matter most?

How much stuff do you require? If you give money to your children for the sole purpose of saving taxes, what does that say to your children? That they are convenient tax deductions? Giving money to the next generation needs greater consideration than just a tax write-off. I have witnessed young children receiving $500 weekly allowances for merely being able to breathe. This can create a sense of entitlement, and the unintended consequences can be dire. Often, these children are never taught appropriate life and financial skills, so they remain dependent on their parents. They may even struggle with major issues later on, like addictions, mental health problems, the inability to hold a real job, and other life challenges.

Talk to your kids about taxes in general, and about how tax policy or incentives shape your business and estate planning. Just as it's healthy to talk about money in age-appropriate ways, it's healthy to talk about where tax money comes from, and what it does in society. It starts when your children begin spending their pocket money and begin to notice simple things like sales tax on their purchases. It continues as you discuss their payroll taxes from their first job (especially if they have sticker shock!), as well as retirement savings and other strategies to reduce taxes and plan for the future. This kind of casual, everyday conversation can make your children more street-smart, and protect them from poor financial advice they may pick up from friends or strangers.

When you have the courage to discuss taxes with your family and plan appropriately, make sure to discuss both sides of the coin. Yes indeed, we regularly witness inefficiencies and waste in government spending, by people we may or may not have voted into office. However, remember that tax revenue also brings value back to the community in the form of infrastructure, education, the military, and first responders. Teaching your kids about taxes goes hand in hand with teaching them about limits, responsibilities, saving, and sharing.

TRUE AND FALSE ADVISORS

Facing the truth about your wealth and your taxes also encompasses finding advisors who have the courage to tell you the truth about what you owe and present you with appropriate solutions. You must be able to trust your advisors' integrity as much as you trust their competence. An overzealous attitude to tax avoidance can make you vulnerable to schemes that promise you a great tax advantage, but ultimately take advantage of you. I've seen such schemes over and over again: Ponzi schemes, selling wine, all kinds of shenanigans that should trip your radar as being too good to be true. The end result is that eventually these schemes are discovered, taxes and penalties are reassessed, and the person who developed the "tax savings opportunity" has unfortunately disappeared.

I once knew an accountant, I'll call him George, who dealt with a lot of successful business owners. His accounting practice included promoting tax shelters that looked fantastic on paper. The amount of tax savings he promised would blow your mind. Clients flocked to him because they didn't want to pay a penny of tax if they could avoid it.

He offered one of these "opportunities" to my husband, but we needed the cash to pay school fees at the time, so he didn't opt in. Months later, we had a tax question, so my husband called George and the receptionist acted a bit strange. She transferred him to the other partner. The partner told him George was dead. What a shocker! How could that be? Was he sick? Did he have a car accident?

All those tax schemes that sounded too good to be true? They were. George was embezzling money from his clients because he had a gambling problem. He'd completely cleaned out a trust that a client had left to care for his wife and children. He blew all the money, and then he blew his brains out in front of his big fancy house. It was awful.

Sometimes a good advisor has to tell you things you don't want to hear and shoot down some of your unrealistic expectations in the process. That's not fun for anyone (including the advisor), but it's part of their commitment to the truth, and you should value it.

If you're presented with an opportunity for a tax shelter that you aren't familiar with or don't understand—even if the person presenting it is your own trusted advisor—I strongly urge you to get a second opinion. Consult other members of your advisory team and get their thoughts. In Chapter Five, we talked about assembling a team of advisors, and this is another good reason why you should work with a team instead of just one person. Even a completely honest person can have limited perspective, make mistakes, or get scammed themselves.

No head of state, whether it's the President of the United States or the Prime Minister of Canada, has just one advisor. Anyone in a powerful position relies on a circle of advisors to ask them the right questions, offer insight, and give them different perspectives on a problem. You couldn't build a house without an architect, general contractor, plumber, carpenter, and so forth—unless you want to live in a makeshift shack. Your family business enterprise and the wealth you have worked so hard to build need and deserve a wealth of good advice to have a secure structure.

If an advisor is unwilling to have their plans vetted, or pushes back on you asking for other opinions, take it from me: that's a red flag. There are many professional advisors who aren't accustomed to a truly collaborative approach, but they shouldn't be secretive or controlling about the way they work with you. Whether it's ego or something more nefarious, be wary of any advisor who discourages you from vetting their plans with someone else—collaboration is key. This does not mean that everyone will be in agreement. The final decision is yours and yours alone. However, different perspectives allow you to think and reflect. Trust your gut when your advisors are giving you varied opinions. Consider the pros and cons and then make a decision. Any decision is better than indecision.

FACE THE CONSEQUENCES

Your tax plan must balance efficiency with complexity and the impact on your family. These elements are like the legs of a stool: if one or two are missing, the whole thing falls down.

When that lopsided stool falls over, the most wrenching consequence is the way it impacts your family and their well-being—both personal and financial. I've seen members of the second or third generation knocked for a loop when the founder—who they always knew as smart, capable, and thoughtful—leaves behind a boneheaded plan, or the chaos of no plan at all. Suddenly, instead of remembering all their parent's or grandparent's admirable traits, they remember them primarily for what they failed to do, and the mess they left behind.

Ultimately, what do you want your legacy to be? Mr. Smith died with $42 million and he had a great tax plan? The whole family is fighting and suing each other, huge swaths of the estate are getting burned up in legal fees, but that tax plan was pristine.

To keep your plans in balance, you need to consider the consequences of tax inefficiency, the consequences of tax efficiency, and the right level of complexity for your family business enterprise (and your stage of life).

> Failing to plan appropriately for your tax obligations can have serious consequences.

INEFFICIENT TAX PLANNING

If your tax planning isn't efficient enough (or you didn't do any at all), your estate might be forced to liquidate some of the assets in your family enterprise in order to pay that tax bill. In this scenario, it's usually the best assets that have to go first, such as selling real estate far below its market value because your heirs need that money quickly in order to clear the estate. When you die and the government comes for its money, nobody wants the dogs in your portfolio. They want your best assets, and they will try to get a great deal.

There's really no excuse for letting your heirs get hit with an unexpected tax bill. You know how much your estate is worth (or you should). It isn't that hard for a competent accountant or tax lawyer to estimate what you will owe. Your eventual death will be sad, and the circumstances may be unexpected, but the fact of death is not a surprise.

The long-term consequences of inadequate tax planning can devastate your dreams for your family legacy. They can wind up dissipating your wealth and erasing all the sacrifices you made to build up that wealth and business in the first place.

FANATICAL TAX PLANNING

Even if you organize your financial affairs in the most tax efficient way possible, the consequences of focusing too much on tax savings can also spin out of control. I've seen this play out in real life, with very ugly consequences for both the family and the wealth creator.

In this instance, a business owner (following the advice of his tax lawyer and accountant) constructed a very elaborate strategy to avoid paying estate taxes on his business. He used corporations, holding companies, and some complex legal footwork to freeze his assets and place them into a trust. Then he made his children and his son-in-law the trustees and beneficiaries of the trust. He was also a beneficiary, but he did not have majority control. Essentially, he owned nothing of that business anymore.

His only condition was that every year, the business would buy him a brand-new Cadillac. Unfortunately, that wasn't in the terms of the trust. It was just a family tradition that had been going on for years.

You can probably guess where this is going. One year, he was advised that he wouldn't be getting a new car because his son-in-law thought it was too extravagant. Of course, he was livid. He'd done all the work to set up this arrangement, paid all the legal fees, and given his entire business to his family, on faith that they would take care of him.

In his indignation, he called up his lawyer to help undo the whole structure. That cost even more legal and accounting fees, and completely destroyed what was otherwise a good family relationship. The fractures extended to his children and grandchildren, so that even cousins stopped speaking to each other.

There's a line between sound tax planning and pushing the envelope so hard that it backfires. That line will be a little bit different for each family and each enterprise, but you need to know where it is, and find advisors who will keep you on the right side of the line and consider the broader impacts of your strategy, beyond tax savings.

CHANGING COMPLEXITY

Back in the eighties I read *Beyond Survival* by Leon Danco, PhD. One of the core concepts in the book is the life cycle of a family business, which he describes in four stages: Wonder, Blunder, Thunder, and Plunder.

In the Wonder stage, you have an idea for a business. You see a problem and think you could create a better solution. Maybe the problem is that you're temperamentally unemployable because you hate being told what to do—many entrepreneurs are! You need to come up with a creative solution to feed yourself. Joking aside, business owners often see a better way of doing things and decide to embark on their own path and start a business.

In the Blunder stage, as you carry on your business journey, you might make a few mistakes along the way. You might choose a bad business partner or make a very expensive business decision that cost more money than your business could afford. Most businesses fail at this stage, because new business owners don't just make ordinary mistakes, they make bigger mistakes than they need to. A mistake that should have cost $500 winds up costing $5,000. Assuming you recover from those mistakes and make it through this stage, the wisdom and skills you acquire will be your path to the next stage.

By the time you reach the Thunder stage, you've honed your skills by trial and error. You know exactly what you have to offer, and you open your eyes every morning determined to be a smashing success. Making all those mistakes and solving all those problems has made you more efficient, and you reach maximum profitability.

In the final phase, Plunder, you really begin to enjoy the fruits of your hard work. Your business is making money for you whether you go to work at 7:00 a.m. or 10:00 a.m. You are receiving the payoff of everything you built.

In your Blunder and Thunder stages, you will naturally have a bigger emphasis on minimizing tax so you can plow more money back into your business and accelerate its growth. Reaching the Plunder stage in your business usually coincides with getting older yourself.

> Your life, your business, and your wealth deserve your attention and intention.

In Chapter Four, we discussed the threshold of complexity and how it changes throughout our lives. At the Plunder stage, it's good to step back and ask yourself what you really want. Forget about taxation, forget estate planning structures. Consider the true purpose of your wealth. Most likely, you have more than you need or want. You are confident that your family will be well taken care of beyond your lifetime. So what is the real purpose of the surplus wealth?

Please don't get me wrong; I'm not against wealth! I'm against mindlessness. I believe, as Socrates said, that the unexamined life is not worth living. Your life, your business, and your wealth deserve your attention and intention.

When I ask clients about the purpose of their wealth, the most common answer I get is *freedom*. They want to be free to support their lifestyle, to help their children, to be free from worry about the future. That's exactly why you need to simplify your plans. Complex tax strategies require a lot of active management, and a lot more hands-on decision-making. A simpler plan may often be better suited to a simpler lifestyle.

Your threshold of complexity isn't the only thing that changes during your lifetime and your business's lifetime. Your assets and tax obligations change, too. As you reexamine your plans, make sure that you regularly update your advisors about the state and scope of your wealth and business enterprise. They need to stay apprised of your holdings, so their planning advice can shift accordingly. We'll talk more about the habit of regular reviews and updates in Chapter Nine.

THE BONUS BOX

On the show *Truth or Consequences*, contestants could choose a drawer from the host's prize box and receive a special bonus. There's a bonus box you can draw on for your tax planning, too. It's one of the simplest and safest ways to preserve the value of your estate, and sometimes it sounds too good to be true: permanent life insurance.

Many people don't understand the powerful role life insurance can play in planning and reducing your estate taxes. Life insurance is a magic tool in this regard. If planned appropriately, it can provide the liquidity your estate needs upon death to meet your tax obligations. When you select the right type of life insurance, you can pay pennies on the dollar for a benefit that will cover your tax bill—it's paying your taxes at a significant discount.

The benefit of proper insurance coverage is easy to understand. When you walk out of life, cash appears, tax-free. It's a beautiful thing to help your family. As we discussed in Chapter One, talking about death is a big taboo, and most people are uncomfortable with it. But when you talk about your death, in essence you're really talking about your values, your legacy, and your hopes and dreams for your family.

Now that you've examined those hopes and dreams, begun to discuss them with your family, found your advisors, and considered your tax position, let's take a look at the next piece of your planning: assessing and managing your human capital risk.

✎ HOMEWORK

- Have you told the truth about the extent of your wealth holdings to yourself, your advisors, and your family? If not, why not?

- What values about taxes do you want to instill in your family? Are your actions backing that up?

- Do you have a scarcity mindset or an abundance mindset? Where do you think that comes from? How has it impacted your tax planning?
- Do your advisors tell you the hard truths you need to hear?
- Have you been tempted to invest in any tax shelters that might be risky or questionable? Where could you get a second opinion about them?
- Which leg of your "stool" (inefficiency, overzealousness, complexity) might need addressing to get your plans in balance?
- Which stage has your business reached in the journey of Wonder, Blunder, Thunder, and Plunder? Are your tax plans suited to your current situation?
- Do you know what your immediate tax obligations will be when you die? Do you know where the money will come from to pay them?

WISE WORDS

"Make your choices reflect your hopes, not your fears."

—*Nelson Mandela*

STRATEGIC ACTION PLAN

Objective:

Due Date:

Why is it important?

What will be the end result?

Who will be responsible for this project?

Who to contact:

Deadline:

Thoughts/Notes:

CHAPTER SEVEN

CONSIDER HUMAN CAPITAL RISK

Bad things happen in life, so you need to be prepared.

Once upon a time, a farmer went into his barn and noticed that one of his geese looked a little...off. He picked her up and saw that she'd laid a very unusual egg. Instead of being white and porous, it was dull yellow and perfectly smooth. He picked up the egg and discovered that it was much heavier than normal. He realized that it was made of solid gold!

He took the egg into town to an appraiser and found that single lump of gold was worth thousands of dollars. The next day, the goose laid another. And the next, and the next. Instead of selling them right away, he decided to collect them and save for the future.

The farmer's collection of solid-gold eggs kept growing, and he soon realized he should protect this amazing asset. He went to his broker and bought an insurance policy for the pile of eggs, but he kept having to update it because the pile kept growing. Nevertheless, the farmer was proud of his foresight in taking out that insurance policy. He patted himself on the back for being a savvy businessman.

He started making plans for how he'd expand his farm, build a new house, upgrade his equipment, and level up his whole operation.

A month or so later, he went into the barn to collect the day's riches and made a tragic discovery. During the night, a fox had broken into the barn and killed the whole flock of geese. Too late, the farmer realized that he'd insured the golden eggs, but he never insured the goose.

As business owners, we are often just as short-sighted as that farmer. We know that we face risks, but we aren't very good at assessing those risks on our own. We insure our cars, our homes, our jewelry, and our business equipment, but we fail to think about the engine that drives our business in the first place—human capital.

We (and the key personnel in our business) are the geese. The business earns money because of what we do. When we stop showing up, the money stops flowing. By all means, insure the eggs! Just don't forget about the goose.

In this chapter, we'll look at human capital risk in general, and the enhanced risk posed to family enterprises. I'll show you ways to mitigate that risk and prepare for an orderly business transition if and when you need one.

WHAT IS HUMAN CAPITAL RISK?

Business risk management is a huge topic, and a comprehensive look at risk management would take up a whole book on its own. For now, I want to focus on one particular type of risk—human capital. Why is this important? Because a business can't operate without people, and it certainly can't prosper without trustworthy, effective, inspiring, and engaging leadership! People are its human capital. These are the risks posed to your business by human nature itself. There's a saying that bad things happen to good people. Well, bad things happen to bad people, too. Bad things happen randomly. All of us, good or bad, will get sick at some point, and eventually die. We are also subject to human emotions and frailty. Partners or family members disagree and sometimes have irreconcilable differences. Marriages break up. Siblings become estranged. All of these events could potentially damage or destroy your business, so you need plans in place to protect it.

People are your human capital.

When most people think about risk, they think of life insurance—and that's a good starting point. Why? Because there is 100 percent certainty that each of us will die. What will happen to your business and family when you do?

In my own family history, we have a perfect example of using life insurance to protect your enterprise and your loved ones. My grandfather, along with his brothers, owned a very successful belt manufacturing business in the 1950s. This was a time when manufacturing in Montreal and New York City was at its peak. The economy was flourishing, jobs were plentiful, and profits were flowing.

As part of prudent financial security and business planning, the brothers secured life insurance on each partner and had a written agreement that in the event of their death, the shares of the business would return to the surviving shareholders. The life insurance proceeds would be used to pay the widow for the value of the deceased partner's shares. When my grandfather passed away suddenly from a brain aneurysm at the age of forty-eight, he had just finished building his dream home (accompanied by a mortgage).

My great-uncles loved my grandmother dearly, but they didn't want her as a business partner. After all, she had no experience or knowledge of the business. With the life insurance proceeds, she was able to pay off the mortgage on their home, bring up her children, and live very comfortably until the age of ninety-four. We should all be so lucky.

It wasn't really all down to luck. My grandfather and his brothers had the foresight to draw up a shareholder agreement with specific provisions, one of which was for the death of a shareholder and the mandatory sale of shares. They also had the foresight to fund that buyout with the purchase of a life insurance policy. If your business lasts long enough, it will outlive all your original shareholders. Having life insurance in place is just common sense.

However, comprehensive risk management goes far beyond life insurance. You might be at the pinnacle of your success and personal productivity when you suddenly get bad news about your health, or you have a catastrophic incident like a stroke that takes you out of commission. Life insurance won't help run your business while you recover, or in case of long-term disability. It also won't help protect your business's financial stability if you or another shareholder wind up getting divorced. Protecting your human capital encompasses protecting your ability to work and earn income, as well as protecting your business from the loss of key people or a breakdown in the boardroom.

YOU ARE THE KEY PERSON

There are a handful of people in your business (usually two or three) who are instrumental to your business's success. You might be able to get by without them for a few weeks, but if they were gone for a few months (or forever), your business might be financially impacted more than you think. You might wind up needing to lay people off due to loss of revenue, or due to increased expenses and mistakes. Those are your key people.

The number one key person is **you**.

As the founder of a business, you are the person who brings everything together, especially in the early years. Have you ever walked into a theatre or concert hall when an orchestra is tuning up? They're all honking and scraping and tweaking—it's chaotic and sounds horrible. Then Maestro comes in and brings everyone together in perfect harmony to perform beautiful music. That's the entrepreneur at work.

> **You are unique and irreplaceable.**

Over the course of the years, you've set the pace for the business to move forward. You've brought some elements forward for emphasis. You've brought new people in and developed the themes of the business in new directions. You keep every part in balance to produce a wonderful outcome. Your contribution is unique and inimitable.

In my thirty-some-odd years of working with business owners, I've found that, by and large, founders are the most hardworking and humble individuals you'll ever meet. They don't think they're important. They give credit to their team and believe, "This business can run itself."

Sound familiar? This is one of the same myths we discussed in Chapter One, that holds people back from making legacy plans at all. And again, I must ask: if your business runs itself, why are you showing up at 6:30 in the morning? Why are you in the office all day and taking calls on the weekends?

Sometimes, clients will still push back and say, "Well, it could run without me, but it wouldn't be as profitable."

You know what they call a business that doesn't make profit? A hobby.

You're the key that makes your business profitable. You're the rainmaker. Sports teams insure their players because they have a unique ability. Business owners have unique abilities, too. They have vision—they can look into the future and see possibilities no one else could. They are the deal makers. They are exceptional problem solvers. They're resilient, because they think creatively. You are unique and irreplaceable, so you need to make a plan that will smooth out the gaps when you can't be there.

BUSINESS STAGES AND RISK STAGES

Throughout the business stages of Wonder, Blunder, Thunder, and Plunder, your risks evolve. In the Wonder and Blunder stages, you accumulate debt. While you're still learning from trial-and-error, you need to insure yourself to provide money and cash flow in the event of your death, disability, or critical illness. That will protect your family from the consequences of any costly mistakes along the way.

In the Thunder stage, your business has grown to the point that you rely on a more comprehensive team. Each key person on your team becomes a golden goose for your business. Your risk expands to include those key personnel, because they're integral to continuing on this profitable trajectory.

When you reach the Plunder stage, your risk exposure is even more complex. Life insurance, though essential, is only one piece of the puzzle. Your most important task to address human capital risk is to make a comprehensive plan to transition your business to new leadership, along with insuring your key people (your flock of golden geese) against death, disability, and critical illness.

At every stage, you encounter risk, and you need to address and mitigate that risk. Whether it's a temporary or permanent health issue, an accident, or even if you die too soon—you need to make sure you don't leave a pile of unpaid taxes, debts, or illiquid assets, so your family will still be taken care of. Putting risk mitigation in place for your human capital should be as automatic as having airbags in your car. Insurance isn't a religion: you don't have to believe in it to buy it.

THE ALPHABET EFFECT

When a business owner dies or becomes disabled for a long period of time, it impacts all the people and businesses they're connected with. This is sometimes known as the Alphabet Effect:

- **A**ccountants start combing through the financial records and preparing final personal and estate tax returns.
- **B**ankers may pull up the line of credit or call in loans.
- **C**reditors start calling. Thirty-, sixty-, or ninety-day payment terms are void; they want their money right now.
- **D**ebtors who owe money go into hiding. They hope that a mess has been left behind so that they can get out of paying until someone sorts it all out.

- Employees get nervous. They may feel that the business isn't stable anymore and jump ship just when the business needs their knowledge and experience the most.
- Family members are looking for the paycheck to arrive. They may not understand that with the owner gone, there may not be any more paychecks.
- Government expects to get their tax payments, either on time and in full, or with penalties for lateness. That includes the regular business and payroll taxes, as well as estate tax and capital gains tax.

You have to put on your big-kid shoes and prepare for these eventualities. Your success isn't just about you and your family. You make an important impact in the economy and the lives of other families, too. Remember the Rockefeller family motto: "For every right implies a responsibility; every opportunity, an obligation; every possession, a duty."

YOUR SPOUSE IS A KEY PERSON

Some entrepreneurs forget how instrumental their family is to the family business, especially if their spouse is a stay-at-home parent. Well, if your spouse gets sick, who is going to drive them to the hospital for treatments? Who will make dinner? Who will take the kids to soccer and football and dance? Who will look after the house? You enjoy your comfortable lifestyle because of a lot of work behind the scenes, and if that major contributor is on hiatus, you will either need to fill the gaps yourself and miss work, or hire help to fill in. There is a huge financial impact when the spouse of a business owner gets sick.

> **For an entrepreneur who works countless hours, a supportive spouse is the foundation and glue that holds the family and business together.**

Some people refer to a stay-at-home spouse as the CEO, or Chief Emotional Officer. When spouses work together as a strong family team, they complement each other to keep the family healthy and happy.

A homemaker is one of the most undervalued human capital assets in any family. To put it in the coldest economic terms, the loss of that person, either temporarily or permanently, will increase your cost of living and decrease your ability to be productive at work. To put it in human terms, if your life partner is critically ill or you lose them altogether, it's devastating and turns your whole life upside down.

I once worked with a couple in this very situation. He was a business owner, and she'd left her professional job to work in administration for the business. They both made the decision to secure a full range of insurance—life, disability, critical illness, and so forth. They came to me for a business audit and intended to cancel some of their insurance policies (which I advised against). We were going to have one more meeting to go over the audit results and make their final decision.

We never made that meeting. She collapsed in the shower, was rushed to the hospital, and was diagnosed with a brain tumor at age fifty-two.

When your loved one is diagnosed with a dire illness, it draws a line in your life: before and after. You go through shock, disbelief, denial, anger, and all the stages of grief. I was very glad that this couple cancelled that final meeting instead of canceling their policies, because I was able to deliver the husband a check in excess of a million dollars to help with their expenses and the loss of both their incomes while they dealt with this diagnosis.

As an initial, knee-jerk reaction, because he wanted to be there for his wife, the husband contemplated selling his business. Because he had money provided by the insurance policies to buy time and think, I was able to convince him to wait. The disability and critical-illness insurance proceeds took the financial pressure off, so he was able to find a solid candidate to run the business in his absence and offer them a competitive salary without a second thought.

That key hire was able to carry on the business without my client having to physically be in the office. This did not put additional financial constraints on the business, nor cause the bank to call in lines of credit. They were in a solid financial position.

The owner was able to accompany the love of his life to her numerous medical appointments and stay by her side for everything she was going through. Fortunately, he didn't have to worry about medical bills either. He had the option to explore the best and most advanced treatment options regardless of cost—that's huge. Unfortunately, the money did not solve her critical illness. Sadly, his wife eventually succumbed to cancer and died. However, he had the freedom to be there for her, provide her with first-class medical care, and create meaningful moments together as a family. On top of that, he was able to make a significant charitable donation for brain cancer research.

Because he was able to rely on the insurance proceeds during this critical juncture in their lives, he didn't need to draw out cash from his business, which would have caused cash flow constraints. More importantly, he was able to be present and supportive to his wife, without worrying about the financial pressures of the business. Instead, he was able to maintain his business operations and continue to reinvest to help the business grow and prosper. During this time of tremendous personal instability, his manager continued to not only maintain the business, but grow it as well. When the owner was finally ready to make business decisions again with a clear head and heart, three years after his wife's diagnosis, he was able to sell that business for far more than he ever anticipated.

MANAGING RISK

Mitigating human capital risks in your business is a two-pronged strategy:

1. Avert the risks that you can avoid, by planning comprehensively with good governance, transition, and succession; and
2. Protect yourself from the risks that you can't avoid by providing solid insurance coverage for your key people.

TRANSITION PLANNING

A vital part of mitigating the risk to your human capital is creating a strong shareholder agreement or transition plan. Those plans most commonly go into effect when a shareholder becomes disabled or passes away, so they need to include buyout, replacement hire, or settlement provisions, to name a few. Formulas for determining fair value of the shares are an integral part of these documents. All those provisions need to be properly funded with life, disability, and critical illness insurance.

Management continuity planning also protects your creditworthiness. When bankers make business loans, they often consider three criteria over the business's financials: management, management, and management. A solid business plan on paper is a baseline requirement for lenders. The banker wants to know that the company's leadership is smart and capable. If the bank finds out you're sick or dying, they'll be the first to call in your loan or pull your line of credit.

Transition plans and shareholder agreements are even more important when there is a significant change in circumstances, like the death of a shareholder, family business disputes, or disputes between business partners.

DEATH OF A SHAREHOLDER

Let's say Elaine and George built a business together. They have complementary talents in different areas, and their individual skills allowed them to grow a thriving business. George owned 51 percent of the voting shares, Elaine 49 percent. Their lawyer helped them draw up a detailed shareholder agreement, but (due to confusion over the legal jargon or simple procrastination) they never got around to signing it. It didn't seem that important, because they worked so well together and trusted each other, and were very busy managing a thriving business.

Then one day George dies. In his will, he leaves everything to his wife Susan. That includes his shares in the business.

Instantly, Susan becomes a majority shareholder and the new president of the company. The problem is, Susan doesn't know anything about the business, nor does she care. While George was working and building the business, she managed the household, scheduling, carpool, kids' activities, and family finances while also volunteering in the community. Susan was busy, just like George. They made a great team. Now that she has become a single parent, her home responsibilities have expanded. Her main concern is where the next check is coming from to support her and the children.

Elaine can't make any significant decisions in the business without Susan's approval. Susan's exceptional marriage partnership with her husband doesn't transfer to being an exceptional business partner with Elaine. Personality clashes aside, there is nobody with George's unique skills in his role, and Susan won't agree to add another salary to their costs. She is barely managing to keep things afloat as she attempts to do her role and her late partner's role. She is exhausted and filled with frustration and uncertainty. Industry changes might make it imperative to reinvest in the business and pivot to a new niche, but Susan just wants to keep drawing out profits at the highest rate possible. It doesn't take long for Susan to run the company into the ground.

That unsigned shareholder agreement included the necessity of securing a life insurance policy to provide for an automatic buyout of shares in the event of a shareholder's death. If only Elaine and George had gotten around to signing the insurance policy and the agreement, the outcome would have been entirely different. Instead of shares, Susan would have received a nice fat check for $7 million and been on her way. Elaine would have become sole shareholder and been able to run the business with her years of experience while she looked for someone to help replace George's lost skills.

SHAREHOLDER DISPUTES

Here's a different scenario: George and Elaine built their business together, and then they come into a major conflict that makes it impossible for them to continue working together. It isn't just a judgment call, but a serious misalignment of values. Perhaps the economy tanks, the business is hard-hit, and they have to invoke austerity measures. They regretfully lay off employees. They ask their remaining staff to take a temporary pay cut.

In the middle of that, George decides that his number one priority is a lavish renovation to his private office bathroom. Their workers are feeling the pinch, but he's frittering money away. He won't listen to reason. Elaine can't overrule him, and he's willing to blow up their partnership if he doesn't get his own way. Elaine needs a structure to help settle this dispute, or she needs an exit strategy. A well-crafted shareholder agreement would provide both.

A solid transition plan will include provisions for different scenarios, whether it be shareholder dispute management, death or disability of a partner, or that the principal hands over control temporarily or permanently. A transition plan (supported by a written and signed document) can help protect a viable business enterprise and provide for a smooth transition.

Paperwork that doesn't seem important day to day can become immensely important overnight. Sadly, these vital documents often get pushed aside and forgotten. The result is a disaster that could have been avoided with one stroke of the pen.

That's the reason it's so important to me that you, the client, understand *why* you need to mitigate your risks, and *why* your plans are structured a certain way. When you clearly see how careful planning (and execution of your planning) can solve the worries that keep you up at night, you will be motivated to follow through and make sure everything is done properly. If you need a parachute, you have to have it packed and loaded *before* you get on the plane. When the plane is going down, it's already too late. The time to draw up shareholder agreements, sign them, and secure them with appropriate insurance is when the relationship is strong and your future is bright.

HOW TO SELECT THE RIGHT INSURANCE

Many people have outdated ideas about buying insurance. They picture some somber-looking door-to-door salesperson, dragging a coffin behind them and trying to instill the fear of God in people. Maybe you encountered someone who tried to overwhelm you with emotional horror stories, and the whole experience was miserable. Quite frankly, it doesn't have to be like that.

Insurance is a tool for human capital risk management. It may also be used as an innovative financial instrument. There are some types of insurance, like critical illness or short- and long-term disability, that you hopefully may never need to claim on. With life insurance, you know that it will pay out eventually. Unfortunately, it's when you die. Essentially, you're buying money at a discount. Depending on the type of policy, you could wind up paying 20 or 30 cents on the dollar to wipe out your outstanding business debts, pay estate taxes, and provide income for your family when you are no longer there.

> Insurance is a tool for human capital risk management.

LIFE INSURANCE

Even if you live to be a hundred, the blessing of long life can bring additional risks to your business and your wealth. As we discussed in Chapter Three and Chapter Six, as long as you continue to build a profitable business, and hold wealth in various appreciating assets, you are likely to create a significant estate tax obligation upon your death. Tax planning may initially reduce some of this liability or defer some of it to other family members, but it can't be eliminated altogether. Death and taxes go hand in hand. Life insurance is a sophisticated financial instrument that provides cash at a significant discount to fund the estate taxes created by your success. Life insurance proceeds can provide time and liquidity to ensure your family legacy goals and preserve the wealth you worked so hard to build. This cash can be used to prevent the forced sale of illiquid family wealth (particularly real estate holdings and operating businesses). And because you bought that money for pennies on the dollar, you wind up significantly reducing the tax burden on your estate.

People often think that life insurance is expensive. That all depends on the type that you select. For example, at first glance group creditor insurance usually seems less expensive than individual term coverage. However, the premiums are not guaranteed, the coverage is not portable if your health changes and you change financial institutions, and there are many other factors that affect the coverage.

In the industry, we refer to term life insurance as rental insurance. Term life insurance is often used to cover temporary debt created by a business, like mortgages or business lines of credit. Term life insurance won't help you with estate tax planning because it usually expires before you do. Standard insurance terms are between ten and twenty years, and your coverage often expires at age seventy.

Permanent insurance, on the other hand, lasts over your whole lifetime. Permanent insurance may sometimes be considered expensive at first glance. However, there are different types of permanent insurance policies. Some contracts have guaranteed premiums, guaranteed cash values, as well as an opportunity to participate in the insurance company's profits. Other permanent contracts offer guaranteed premiums with no fallback position in the event of an unpaid premium. Reviewing the different elements of any insurance proposal requires discernment and expertise.

LIVING BENEFITS

Some people feel that the prospect of chronic sickness is worse than death. This is because when someone is not well, the inability to work and earn an income, coupled with increasing medical costs, can feel overwhelming. After all, the last thing you want or need when you're sick is to incur more debt—especially if you don't know whether or how you could pay it back. There are two sources of income: you working, or money working for you. There are two types of insurance that can put money to work when you aren't able to work: critical illness and disability insurance.

Critical illness insurance covers you in the event of a life-threatening health event. A typical critical illness policy will pay out $250,000 to $5 million if you have a heart attack, stroke, life-threatening cancer, or other major health problem. It provides a lump sum payment, with no conditions attached on receipt of the check, so you can use the money any way you want. I've seen people use this money for extra nursing care, pet care, vacations, clearing a mortgage, hiring household help, and many other means of making their life easier while dealing with their health situation.

A critical illness policy may also be secured by the business on a key employee. This will create funds for the business to hire a replacement in the event of the temporary loss of a key person due to cancer, stroke, or a heart attack. This alleviates financial pressure on your business while the business deals with its own challenging transition.

Disability insurance covers you in the event of a long-term disability, whether from sickness or an accident. As compared to critical illness insurance that pays out a lump-sum benefit, disability insurance payments are more like a steady stream of money to replace loss of income. This stream of payments can be used to support the disabled employee and prevent an additional cash drain on the business. I don't know about you, but if I'm sick—really, really sick and unable to work—I'd rather use someone else's money than rely on my hard-earned investments and wealth.

Many business owners think they can self-insure for this type of crisis. That's not a good idea. Oftentimes, there is so much debt at an early point in our businesses that there's very little wiggle room to take on additional debt and risk. When the business is profitable, there can still be major financial repercussions if a key person or business owner is unable to work due to sickness or accident. More often than not, successful businesses take on debt to turn it into equity. If the owner happens to get sick at a time when they've taken on significant debt to expand the business, their financial stability can go down like a house of cards.

Later, when we have more capital in reserve, business owners believe insurance is unnecessary and there are sufficient retained earnings to cover this risk. Remember though, that insurance leverages your money. Self-insuring is always an option, but of course you lose the "discount" effect of paying pennies on the dollar for coverage.

The process of examining your risks and protecting yourself from unforeseen events will support a strong financial position for your business and ultimately yourself. Putting a plan in place to mitigate these risks gives you more stability when things go wrong. A well-qualified, insurance-specialized financial advisor can help you assess your risk today and look ahead to every stage of your business and life, to match you with the type and amount of protection you require. The right insurance protection can keep bad news from turning into a disaster for your business and your wealth.

KEY PEOPLE TO INSURE

You probably have fire insurance in case your building caught fire. What about protecting your human capital? The best risk mitigation strategy thinks about people, not just about things. Family enterprises often employ one or two key people who contribute to the growth and profitability of a business. Their leadership and skills are integral, since their contribution often provides the founder with freedom of time. If you can identify key people whose sudden absence would jeopardize the financial stability of your business, you may want to consider key person insurance coverage.

Consider who is really making your organization run. Which members of your team would be the hardest to replace if they got hit by a bus tomorrow? Which ones would you need to replace most urgently? Whose long-term absence would cause significant financial losses?

They might be a star CFO, marketing director, your general

manager, or a member of your leadership team. What is their full replacement cost? Obviously, you can't "replace" a human being, but you need to think deeply about everything they do, and how you can fill those gaps if they're out of commission, either temporarily or due to premature death or disability.

If anything were to happen to them, you'd need to have money available quickly so you could pay top dollar for a high-quality interim or permanent replacement, because you can't let that gap derail your business. That's what key person insurance is all about: the business receives money in the event of the key person's death or disability, to ensure business stability. Their total coverage with life, critical illness, and disability insurance should amount to four to six times their compensation.

Key person insurance plans are normally pennies on the dollar. Isn't it worth a tiny percentage of your revenue to guarantee that your operations could continue smoothly if an unforeseen death or disability hit one of your key people?

NO EXCUSES

I hear a lot of excuses from clients who resist taking out appropriate disability, life, and critical illness coverage. I'm here to tell you, those excuses are all hogwash.

Here's one: *My expenses will go down if I'm sick.*

To a certain degree, illness and disability reduce people's lifestyles. They aren't traveling, going out on the boat, buying a car, spending time at the cottage, or entertaining. But those restrictions don't translate into saving money!

The truth is the exact opposite: your expenses go *up*. You'll have medical expenses, regardless of how wonderful your private or public coverage may be. You may require modifications to your home to make it more comfortable and accessible. Unless you already have qualified household help with training for home nursing care, you'll probably need to hire help to take care of routine tasks that you would normally do for yourself. You might consider a family member as a caregiver, but they can't do it alone. They will need support, too. This additional support costs money.

Assuming that you recover and go back to work, do you want to be forced to go back as soon as humanly possible? Or would you rather have the option to spend quality time with your family and enjoy your renewed lease on life? You can't look your mortality in the eye on a Friday and go back to the office Monday like nothing happened. Catastrophic experiences change you, and they change your priorities.

Here's another: *I won't get sick.*

This is the Superman myth all over again. Listen, it's normal for teenagers to believe they're bulletproof—after all, they're young and naive. As you journey through life, it's incredible how we hear stories of people we know experiencing health hiccups, being diagnosed with cancer, and other life tragedies. The reality is there's a point at which optimism becomes denial. I have yet to hear of anyone getting sick or dying at the "right time." It just doesn't happen.

If we have to go, we'd all prefer for it to be quick and painless—while we're sleeping or instantaneously as we're doing something we love. But that's not the reality for most people. For most of us, death or disability often follows a slow decline that sucks you into a vortex of tests, treatments, bills, sleepless nights, isolation, and pain. If we're lucky we can escape that slow suffering, but luck is for lotteries. Insurance isn't a lottery. It's risk management. It's just good business. Buying insurance is like planting a tree—the best time to plant a tree was twenty years ago, and the second-best time is today. The worst time to secure insurance is after you've been to the doctor and received bad news, because then it's too late.

> Human capital is the foundation of your financial well-being, success, and financial independence.

Your key people (including yourself) keep your business flowing. Your physical and mental health enable you to have a big future. Without them, your future and your family's future can crumble right in front of you.

BE PREPARED

Your financial advisors should be able to conduct a risk audit for your enterprise (ideally, they would do these audits on a regular basis). They should examine each aspect of your human capital risk exposure and make sure you have an appropriate mitigation strategy in place.

> Managing risk is the definition of disaster-proofing your legacy, both business and personal.

Once again, the initial meeting with your advisor should involve deep discovery of how your business runs, current resources available, the key people involved, and what is keeping you awake at night, as well as a number of curious and thought-provoking questions that you may not have considered before. For example, what would happen to the business if a key person died or became sick and was unable to work? What if this were temporary? What if this were permanent?

Engaging in a conversation with an advisor who is curious, resourceful, responsive, and most importantly, attentive will help you clarify your goals and your blind spots and consider all possible alternatives. Once they understand your goals, vision, and values, the advisor will examine your life and disability coverage, as well as employee benefits. They'll want copies of all your insurance contracts to see if there are any gaps. They'll assess which policies should be personally or corporately held. They'll make you aware of any contract exclusions, and any terms that might expire while you still need coverage. Then they can tailor their advice to your situation. A smart advisor doesn't have all the answers, they just ask good questions.

I urge you to find an advisor you can rely on to help you with this, rather than trying to audit your coverage yourself. They will have a process specifically designed to help you identify your planning gaps (if any) as well as ensure that the correct policies are in place. You wouldn't self-diagnose a tooth cavity or chest pain—you'd go to a dentist or doctor and submit to their diagnostic process. At the same time, if your doctor tried to hand you a prescription without asking you anything about your symptoms, your health, or your family history, you probably wouldn't have a high degree of trust and confidence in that diagnosis. You might want a second opinion. Likewise, if an advisor tries to hand you a prepackaged strategy without asking you questions and reviewing what you currently own, learning about your situation and goals, then quite frankly, that's not an advisor you should rely on.

Managing risk is the definition of disaster-proofing your legacy, both business and personal. Your human capital and the talent you employ are the heart of your enterprise. Being prepared for an orderly transition if an unforeseen event occurs to you or your key people will enable you to keep the heart of your business beating.

It's not enough to make plans in your mind or talk them out with your advisors. You have to make sure your plans and wishes are documented and executed properly. In Chapter Eight, we'll discuss everything you need to get in writing.

HOMEWORK

Let's do a thought exercise to create your disaster recovery plan.

Bang! You're dead.

Tomorrow morning, who's going to do what you do in your business? Does anyone even know what to do?

Identify your key people, including yourself. How much money would you need, and how much does the business need, if they were unable to work?

What is your operating line of credit? Is it insured?

List any current business loans. Are they properly insured?

The second part of this homework isn't a thought exercise; it's practical. Gather together all your insurance contracts, whether they cover you personally or your business assets, and put them in a file. Don't worry about looking at them yet, just collect them. Then call your current advisor or interview some new advisors to find out whether they have a coherent process to help you discover your risks and any gaps in your coverage. Have them explain their process and determine if it speaks to you in a way that makes a difference. Are they curious, resourceful, alert, responsive? Find out how they work, and what measurable result you can expect at the end of the process.

WISE WORDS

"The most serious failure of leadership
is the failure to foresee."

—*Robert Greenleaf, founder,*
Greenleaf Center for Servant Leadership

STRATEGIC ACTION PLAN

Objective:

Due Date:

Why is it important?

What will be the end result?

Who will be responsible for this project?

Who to contact:

Deadline:

Thoughts/Notes:

CHAPTER EIGHT

GET IT IN WRITING

Your legacy planning includes legal documents and personal instructions to make sure your family isn't left in the dark.

A very successful wealth builder had three daughters. As a working mother with only an eighth-grade education, she had used her innate drive and photographic memory to educate herself and build a successful family enterprise alongside her spouse. She lived frugally, never paying retail for anything. She studied the stock market, saved and invested wisely, and created a significant legacy for her children. We are talking eight figures here.

Each of her daughters got married and had children. Along the way, their mother bought each of them a house to give them a good start in life. Unfortunately, two of the daughters wound up divorcing their husbands, and because the houses were not protected by marital agreements, the value was divided and lost to the ex-husbands. The mother hated to see that hard-earned money wasted and resolved to protect her children's fortune more carefully.

When she died, all her money was placed in a trust for tax purposes. The three daughters were co-trustees, entitled to equal shares, and the terms of the trust extended to let their children take over as trustees and beneficiaries when one died. Beyond that, there were very few rules on how the proceeds of the trust should be used, and no provision for settling disputes. None of that seemed necessary to the founder because she knew that her daughters all got along and communicated well with each other. She had faith in their ability to work things out among themselves.

Indeed, the system worked perfectly for many years. The sisters discussed the use of the trust money among themselves, accessed what they needed when they needed it, and were satisfied that the distributions evened out over time. There was a deep sense of trust and mutual respect among the three siblings like nothing I had ever witnessed before.

Then one sister died, and things started to get complicated. Her children inherited her share of the trust and became co-trustees. Now there were five people trying to work together to make decisions about distributions, investments, and needs—with wildly varying expectations, expertise, and requirements.

Suddenly, there was conflict. The easy give-and-take among the three siblings did not extend to the next generation. Although the original beneficiaries never thought about counting and sharing distributions down to the exact dollar, the nieces and nephews (and their respective spouses) had different ideas. The daughters were confident that their mother's intent was for the trust to be distributed in thirds, so the nieces and nephews should all split a one-third share. The trouble was that this system was not clarified in the trust document itself. The nieces and nephews, as co-trustees and beneficiaries, believed that the trust should now be split into equal shares for each beneficiary: six shares instead of three. There were also disagreements over what sort of distributions the trust should make, how the money should be used, how the investments should be decided, and so forth. Again, there were no provisions in the trust documents to settle these questions.

Over time, as each of the daughters passed away and their children stepped up as co-trustees, things got more and more contentious. It's impossible for twelve people to share the same mindset and perspective without any rules or framework for their decisions.

Everyone was convinced that they understood the founder's wishes. Everyone was convinced that their idea was the fairest and most equitable arrangement. Without a shared set of rules and values, the trust was left vulnerable to manipulation and unfair handling—or at least, to accusations of unfairness. Every decision was open to misinterpretation that generated more conflict and hostility. Despite a lifelong harmony and goodwill among the family members, these disagreements became disputes that threatened to tear the family apart.

All this because the founder didn't put her wishes in writing. She executed legal documents for her estate plan, but those documents lacked the clarity and intentionality they needed to hold up over time. There was no mention of history, values, purpose, or charity. There was no roadmap to extend the founder's legacy beyond the second generation.

What is the true purpose of your wealth? What does your money mean to you, your family, and your community? If it just means the accumulation of stuff and spending on a whim, you'll soon have no money and no family cohesion either. In order for your legacy to extend beyond your lifetime, you must ensure that your values, vision and goals are transmitted along with it. Otherwise, your experience, priceless wisdom, and true intentions will be lost. You will have robbed future generations of well-being, guidance, direction, and the incredible impact they could be making in the world.

As you work with your team of advisors to draw up your estate plans, there are certain legal papers you'll need, like your will, your powers of attorney, and perhaps a trust or marital agreement. Over and above those formal documents, you also need to record your wishes and intentions. Your family needs to understand what your planning decisions mean, how you came to these decisions, and why you have organized your planning in this particular way. They will need a written reminder to ensure that message doesn't get diluted or lost over time. Lastly, you should set up a specific location where your family can access all the documents and information they need in one place.

YOUR WILL AND YOUR WISHES

My grandfather passed away of a brain aneurysm at the young age of forty-eight. I never met him. Apparently, he was a hardworking, generous and kind man. Years ago, rummaging through old files at my parents' home, I read my grandfather's will. It started off, "To my beloved wife Libby, I leave…"

If you asked ten people to look at the first three lines of their wills today, I'd give you a hundred dollars if you found the word "beloved." The vast majority of wills I have the privilege of reviewing these days are templated, cold, wordy documents that don't demonstrate who the testator really is, or what the testator really wants and why. Lawyers default to impersonal, standardized templates because they are easy to use, save time, and often use legalese that they believe a judge will understand. Do you think they are getting prepared for an estate litigation case? Perhaps. There's some benefit to starting with a template to make sure everything gets included and the legal language is unquestionably correct—but after all, that's what you're paying the lawyer to do! Does this document truly convey to those you love who you are and what you want?

> Your family needs to understand what your planning decisions mean, how you came to these decisions, and why you have organized your planning in this particular way.

Without some personal insight into the testator's thinking, more often than not the family can't understand the reasons behind their choices. This often leads to divisions, resentment, and family conflict. If that conflict isn't dealt with properly, it can even lead to litigation. Estate litigation is a growing field in the US and Canada (all over the world, really). I'm personally convinced that much of it is driven by a number of factors, including lack of communication when the wealth holder was alive to share the contents of their will, not enough "soft" questions asked by the professional drawing up the document, and a lack of personal expression or wishes in the documents they leave behind.

I've heard horror stories from colleagues about family feuds that could have been avoided with the simplest of precautions. One involved a mother who had done a good job getting her affairs in order as far as her finances went, but never took the time to discuss the disposition of any of her personal belongings. The most contentious was the family dining table, where they had always celebrated Thanksgiving and Christmas. There were so many years of warm memories attached to that table that both siblings wanted to keep it when she passed.

Unfortunately, it seemed that the mother had promised that dining room set to each of her children at different times, so they both expected to receive it. Their family meeting to pack up her house turned into a huge argument, complete with screaming and throwing ashtrays. Instead of coming together to mourn their mother and support each other, they stormed out and haven't spoken to each other since. There was no prior history of conflict between them, but that relationship was permanently damaged—all for the want of a simple conversation and a simple letter that could have documented their mom's wishes.

I encourage my clients—and I encourage you, too—to write out a letter of wishes to accompany their will. A letter like this doesn't need to have all that legal boilerplate in it, and it isn't legally binding. It gives you the opportunity to explain your thinking and your intentions, so that your family can understand and appreciate the decisions you made about your wealth. They need to know that you had their best interests in mind. If you haven't taken the time (or gathered your courage) to initiate conversations about your wealth and treasured heirlooms, then a letter of wishes is key.

The time you spend preparing your will and a letter of wishes is an ideal time to have intentional conversations with your family about your plans. Make sure your executor, the trustees of any trusts you might create, and your family members are familiar with the contents of your will and the approximate size of the estate you're gifting. Most importantly, don't forget to tell them where your will is located! If you think this conversation isn't age-appropriate for your kids, think again. If they're old enough to know what money is and see how you have managed and spent it, then they're old enough to start learning what it means to be responsible for the legacy you're leaving them.

The conversations you have now will lay the groundwork for their understanding and responsible stewardship. A letter of wishes can provide deeper insight, so that your family can fully grasp *how* and *why* this family legacy was created. Combined with stories and lessons learned, that legacy of the heart will extend beyond any amount of money they may receive.

There are resources available to help you write these documents. These services range from professionals in legacy planning to consultants who are experienced in helping wealth holders and individuals manage sudden wealth. If you contact the Purposeful Planning Institute, they can help you find professional advisors with a collaborative, values-driven approach to legacy planning. You can reach the PPI at info@purposefulplanninginstitute.com.

DOES "FAIR" MEAN "EQUAL"?

Planning for your family legacy isn't always straightforward. Every person is unique, and every family is unique with different circumstances. Mixed in with these circumstances are family relationships. Sometimes it's clear that an equal division of the assets in an estate is fair for everyone. In other situations, these variable circumstances mean that an equal split isn't necessarily the wisest or fairest plan. You may have one child who's become very successful in their own right, with a very high income and net worth. Another might work very hard in a noble but underpaid profession. You may have a child or grandchild with special needs or catastrophic health problems, and you may want to consider how to provide for them when they may never be able to support themselves, or they may require long-term care.

You may feel that you should give more support to the child with more significant needs. On the other hand, you may believe that all your children have an equal claim and need to make their own decisions, so it's only right to give them equal shares to ensure family harmony. There's no single right answer to these questions. You have to make the best choices you can according to your own values. It's your money and you have the right to do whatever you want with it. The essential thing is to have ongoing conversations with your family about those values. Also, those conversations need to be a two-way street. Your loved ones need to know that you care about their lives, and you prove that by listening. Open, ongoing communication can make the difference between a family that pulls together in the long run, and one that falls apart.

You may wish to discuss these dilemmas with a third-party professional. Oftentimes, a trusted advisor, be it legal, accounting, or financial, can act as a sounding board before you make any final decisions. Remember, at the end of the day, this is your hard-earned wealth, and ultimately your decision. Do not get swayed by a particular strategy if it impairs what you want to achieve for your family and community.

YOUR LEGACY LETTER

In addition to a letter of wishes that accompanies your will, I highly recommend that you write your family a legacy letter every few years. A legacy letter should be a reflection of your past, including the pearls of wisdom and experience that you have learned from and are grateful for (or not), and that you want to pass on to your children or grandchildren. The biggest gift you could share with them is the lessons you have learned in a lifetime of experience and overcoming challenges. It's a snapshot of your true valuables—the *values* that have provided you direction and strength to achieve the level of wealth and success you now have.

> A legacy letter can help you unravel the mysteries of your own success and provide insight to help your children as they journey through their lives.

I wrote my first legacy letter to celebrate a new decade in my life. It was a wonderful experience, and it made me wish I'd written one every decade of my adult life. Each letter certainly would have been a different story!

I remember the years when our children were young as one long, mad rush from the soccer pitch or hockey arena, to the PTA meeting, to a business conference. One day might start with a 7:30 a.m. business breakfast meeting. Every other week, I'd drive two hours to Montreal for five meetings there. On Fridays, I'd race home from work to try to get Shabbat dinner on the table. We could have all used a break for Mom to think deeply about what I wanted my kids to learn. What values would I impart? Probably the same ones I write to them now: "Work hard, do the best you can, embrace failure as a learning opportunity, be a kind and honest person, and everything will turn out okay."

No doubt your success came at a price. You had to persevere through uncertainty, failure, pain, and perhaps moments of despair.

You needed great courage to take the next step forward. Nobody becomes successful purely through luck (although a little bit of luck certainly helps). You know the saying that luck is preparation, meeting opportunity—and taking action. Every successful venture depends on some measure of luck and timing. A legacy letter can help you unravel the mysteries of your own success and provide insight to help your children as they journey through their lives.

ALL THE PUZZLE PIECES

The list of legal documents you need will differ somewhat if you're a solo business owner, a member of a partnership, or if you have a complex family business enterprise. Let's discuss each scenario:

Every adult needs their personal documents in place.

- A will: a personal will deals with the disposition of all the assets you hold in your own name, such as personal property, retirement accounts, investments, cash, and your home and cars. This personal will must go through probate when you die before those assets can be distributed to the beneficiaries. Probate is a certification from the court that your will is valid, and there are accompanying probate fees.
- General powers of attorney (sometimes called a continuing power of attorney for property).
- A medical directive, which may also be referred to as a living will.
- A medical power of attorney, which may be called a power of attorney for personal care, or a healthcare proxy.

A business owner will need all those personal documents, plus documents related to their business enterprise:

- In some countries or jurisdictions, there can also be a secondary *business will* that deals with your shares and other assets held in businesses and corporations. It does not need to go through probate, which can reduce the amount of probate fees that your estate is obligated to pay and allow the business to keep operating smoothly. If you have significant assets in other countries, there are distinct laws as to transfer of assets, estate taxes, and separate wills to deal with the disposition of those assets.

- Shareholder agreements that include a mandatory buyout provision for situations such as death or disability of a shareholder. We looked at the importance of strong shareholder agreements in Chapter Seven.

- Family business rules that state the policies and principles of the business's governance. We looked at the Family Business Rulebook in depth in Chapter Four.

- Employment agreements for all employees, including the shareholders. Believe it or not, even if you have a shareholder who's also an employee, you need that employment agreement. If you need to buy them out, you'll probably need to fire them, too. If so, you don't want to wind up in court on a technicality.

PERSONAL REPRESENTATIVES

You will need to appoint a variety of personal representatives to handle your affairs should you become ill or incapacitated, as well as those who will administer your estate in the event of your death. A catch-all term for those you entrust to act on your behalf is "fiduciary." A fiduciary has the duty to act in the best interest of the person they represent, or their beneficiaries. Your fiduciaries may include your executors, the trustees of any trusts you create, those who hold power of attorney for you, and the guardians of your minor children.

> Nature abhors a vacuum. If you don't communicate the reason *why* you chose your representatives, your family will draw their own conclusions—which may be wrong and even hurtful.

EXECUTOR

You need to appoint an executor for your will. Be intentional about choosing the right person to be in charge of your affairs, be it a family member, friend, or trusted professional. Being an executor is tedious, time-consuming, and the most thankless job on earth. Every single asset and every debt must be identified and documented. Debts and estate taxes must be paid **before** distributing assets to the designated heirs, or the executor becomes liable for those obligations. Frequently, an executor has to deal with the heirs asking, "Where's my money?" Managing expectations for your heirs at a time when your estate may have tremendous complexity is not easy.

If you distribute too much without paying enough taxes, or if you distribute funds to the wrong person, guess who's on the line?

The executor. Asking someone to be your executor isn't necessarily an honor. It's a complex, stressful, and underappreciated job.

Choose executors who are trustworthy, reliable, and financially literate. They should also know and understand your family members, their needs, abilities, limitations, and mindset. I usually encourage clients to pick more than one person. Executors have a lot of work to do, but they don't make decisions on their own. They follow the directions in your will, keep detailed accounts, and submit everything to the court. If there is insufficient liquidity in your estate, they may be responsible for selling assets to pay estate taxes. Keeping your heirs informed is critical. Once all the assets are properly disposed or distributed to the rightful heirs, the estate is closed, and the executor's job is done.

TRUSTEES

A trustee's job, on the other hand, is ongoing. They need to exercise discretion and make thoughtful, responsible financial decisions that are in the best interest of your beneficiaries. If a trust is created by a provision in your will (referred to as a Testamentary Trust) I really encourage choosing more than one trustee—in fact, I recommend three.

There's a saying that "odds are better than evens," because two trustees in disagreement may inadvertently create a stalemate for decision-making. However, with three appointed trustees, majority rules, so decisions can be made and implemented in a timely and thoughtful fashion. They also bring a broader and deeper understanding of the family's needs. Multiple viewpoints provide varied insights. Perhaps one trustee really understands the beneficiaries, one is very financially savvy, and one deeply understands your feelings and wishes. It could be any configuration, but the point is that having three trustees deepens your bench to make sure all the attributes of a good fiduciary are covered for the benefit, protection and well-being of your heirs.

It's a good idea to build flexibility into a trust document, such as the option to change trustees, in case that becomes necessary in the future. Perhaps one of your children would be the best person to become a trustee when they attain a certain age or level of maturity. They will have the opportunity to learn from experienced trustees, and then gain a seat at the table to have more agency in their own future.

POWERS OF ATTORNEY

You need to appoint a power of attorney for your financial decisions in case you become temporarily or permanently incapacitated. Bear in mind that your financial and medical representatives don't necessarily need to be the same person. In the event that you suffer a catastrophic illness or disability, placing all that responsibility on one person might be too much of a burden. Furthermore, the right person to make medical decisions might not be the right person to make financial decisions. I advise my clients to divide those roles, both to ensure good decision-making and to lighten the toll that responsibility can take on the people you appoint.

GUARDIANS

If your children are minors, you need to choose a guardian as well as an executor and trustees. I also recommend a letter of wishes for your guardians, so that they are not parachuted into becoming parents without some kind of instruction manual. I often see parents boggle at their own choice of guardian when we do a document audit. "I can't believe I chose them! Do you know what he did? We're not even speaking anymore." It's a good idea to revisit your documents every three to five years while your children are growing up, because life and relationships change.

Overall, your choice of fiduciaries comes down to thinking deeply about the people you can rely on, who understand you, and who will take good care of your family. When you start adding all those criteria, the list of friends and relatives who can step into that role gets very, very short.

Sometimes there just isn't anyone you know or believe can fulfill all the responsibilities of a fiduciary, and that's when it's time to look at engaging a lawyer or a bank to act on your behalf. They are neutral, efficient, and accountable. The downside, of course, is that they don't have the intimate knowledge to make personalized decisions based on your family's individual needs. That's when a small group of trustees can be really valuable.

When my husband and I most recently updated our wills, we appointed three executors: a tax lawyer and two of our children. When we let our kids know about the new arrangement, my youngest questioned why she wasn't chosen.

Our reasoning was very simple. It wasn't anything personal. She was in a stage of her life when she traveled a lot and was working abroad. For specific tax purposes in our situation, an executor needed to be a permanent resident, and we wanted someone who was stable in one location instead of moving around frequently. Our estate is going to take a couple of years to settle completely, and our executors need to be available to make sure everything gets done in a timely manner.

It was crucial, however, that we had that conversation and she heard our reasoning from our own lips. It had nothing to do with competency or favoritism, it was a tax efficient and responsible decision. In the aftermath of a death, decisions can be so easily misconstrued. Children can, and often do, internalize this type of choice as a commentary on their character or their ability. "Mom and Dad never thought I was smart enough," or "Everyone thinks I'm the flaky one."

Those judgments could be the furthest thing from your mind, but nature abhors a vacuum. If you don't communicate the reasons for your choices, your children will draw their own conclusions, and those conclusions are apt to be wrong and hurtful.

TRUSTS

A trust is essentially a bucket that holds assets. Make sure you are clear about the purpose of the trust **before** you sign the document. This document cannot be modified without significant complexity including costs and court approval. I have yet to see a trust document altered.

A trust may hold investments such as shares of a business, stocks, real estate and cash. Trusts may be created while you are living (inter vivos) or upon your death (testamentary). When you transfer assets into a trust, you are no longer the legal owner of those assets. The assets are put aside for the designated beneficiaries of your choosing. The income and capital may be distributed among the beneficiaries as per the provisions of the trust documents and at the discretion of the trustees. The capital and income earned from the trust can only be used as the trust document directs, for the stated purpose of the trust, such as supporting the beneficiaries, paying for their education and well-being, and so forth.

If your estate plan includes a trust, construct it thoughtfully and make sure you understand all of the options open to you. In Canada, trusts are limited to twenty-one years after the initial inception. In the US trusts can run for much longer—up to one hundred years, or in some cases, in perpetuity. The beneficiaries of a trust can be your family members, corporations, charities, or whomever you decide. Make sure your planning and trust document include some flexibility, and don't get so starry-eyed thinking about future generations that you forget to provide for your own needs. I've heard real-life versions of *King Lear* where a business founder entrusted all their assets to their children and grandchildren (to save taxes) and wound up out in the cold instead of being cared for.

I recommend including a letter to explain why you have created this trust for your beneficiaries and guide them in being good stewards of your family values. Remember, valuables (financial gifts) can be misappropriated, misused, or disappear. Values are a compass for good choices and last forever.

MARITAL AGREEMENTS

Prenuptial agreements are a topic nobody likes to think about, because nobody likes to think about divorce. But it happens, and with the current divorce rate, it's something every couple needs to consider. Let's get real, this is a difficult and uncomfortable subject. It needs to be handled in a respectful, sensitive way so that an engaged couple doesn't feel that their relationship is tainted before they've even started building their future together.

However, the couple needs to understand that by entering into a marriage where there is business ownership or significant wealth tied up in assets with other family members, a dissolution of that marriage can have a severe impact on many other families—not just their own. Think of a marriage contract like storing a fire extinguisher in your kitchen. You hope you never need it, but if anything goes wrong, you'll be glad you have it.

MARRIAGE AND DIVORCE

I think the best advice I ever give my clients is to choose their spouse wisely. This advice does not guarantee the longevity of a relationship by any means. It simply brings to their attention that relationships take work. And often, even with work, relationships may not last. That being stated, the reality is that (according to the United States census) over 40 percent of first marriages end in separation or divorce. Nothing is guaranteed in life with the unfortunate exception of death and taxes.

An emotional, acrimonious divorce can destroy a business, which may impact the livelihood of the families the business employs, force liquidation of assets below their actual value, and set off a domino effect of destruction. I've seen the emotional and financial carnage from marriages that don't work, and the fallout from having so many volatile emotions wrapped up in a settlement agreement. Unfortunately, too few of these couples were able to put their personal conflicts aside and settle things amicably. There have been some exceptions, but it's not the norm.

When you prepare shareholder agreements (especially in partnership situations), you need to make sure there are provisions that protect the business in the event of a divorce. There's a saying among family lawyers and therapists: you have to love your kids more than you hate your ex. In this context, it means that you have to keep your family's long-term best interests in mind. Owning a business impacts more than just the married couple and the family. There are many people depending on the business for their security and livelihood: employees that are feeding their own families, suppliers, customers, and the list goes on. Every shareholder in the business—whether they are your original business partner or a family member—needs their interests protected.

No one is ever fully prepared for the emotional and financial onslaught of a divorce, any more than they can be prepared for the illness or death of a beloved spouse or child. All of those situations can leave you numb and unable to function. If you aren't capable of making the urgent daily decisions that keep your business running, it doesn't take long for that business to run off the rails. I've seen family businesses go into bankruptcy just because the owner took their eyes off their business for a short time while they were grieving.

Money doesn't mend a broken heart or replace the person who's gone, but it can buy you time to think and heal. Legal documents can't keep a marriage together, but well-structured planning can minimize the financial tsunami in some ways.

> **A prenup isn't cheap—emotionally or financially—but it's cheaper than a messy divorce on both fronts.**

A marriage contract can be as simple or complex as you want it to be. It may be as simple as stating that in the event of a divorce, all assets are divided equally among the two parties. It may be as complex as excluding designated assets from any future settlement.

In basic terms, a marital agreement often stipulates that each person keeps whatever they had before the marriage, and specifies which particular assets are separate or shared in the event of a divorce. There may be clauses regarding child and spousal support, and under what circumstances. This can be particularly important when there is generational wealth because the agreement can govern gifts to a spouse from their parents.

Importantly for a family business, a properly worded marriage contract excludes business shares and other illiquid family assets from being sold at fire sale prices. Remember the story of George, Elaine, and Susan from Chapter Seven? I've seen it play out in real life, with thriving businesses ending in bankruptcy because of a spouse's rights to the shares. Indeed, some shareholder agreements specify that any member of the business entity must have a marital agreement that excludes the business's shares from the marital property. Otherwise, if one spouse has to buy out the other's interest in the business, it could impoverish the business to write that check. A sound marital agreement doesn't just protect the couple. It protects every shareholder and employee involved in that business by ensuring the business remains stable and secure to continue operating.

Whatever matrimonial agreement you design and implement, the process of discussing and planning enables the couple to have an informed and meaningful talk about their beliefs, the impact of their marriage upon others, and an opportunity to have a conversation about money and values. Since money problems are one of the biggest causes of divorce, it's always good to get on the same page earlier rather than later.

Marital agreements are yet another "pay me now or pay me later" situation. Is it better to have these discussions with a lawyer when both partners are happy and in love, or to pick through financial statements with a lawyer when everyone is emotionally charged, angry, and resentful? A prenup isn't cheap—emotionally or financially—but it's cheaper than a messy divorce on both fronts. It's a necessity.

YOUR FAMILY DESK REFERENCE

No one enjoys rummaging through filing cabinets, office drawers, boxes, or computer drives during a time when they are also grieving the loss of a loved one. It's a needlessly burdensome chore that amplifies your family's pain, confusion, and potential conflict.

Your wealth holdings may be complicated, but your recordkeeping doesn't need to be. A family desk reference is a manual that contains everything your loved ones need to know in order to take care of your affairs if you're incapacitated or when you die. It can be an electronic document or a simple three-ring binder; it can even be a handwritten list on a legal pad. It doesn't matter what your system is like. What matters is that you collect everything in one place, that the information is accurate and readable, and that your family knows where to find it.

I suggest creating one three-ring binder with various sections. Put in a summary of information about your personal assets, businesses, and investments, as well as copies of your estate planning documents. The binders will need to be updated regularly as your family and circumstances change, and we'll discuss that more in Chapter Nine. The binders are a simple system to keep a list of what you have and where everything is, so those updates are easier to keep on top of.

I encourage you to begin your binder with what I call "A Letter of Wishes." This letter should explain your purpose in the way you've planned your estate and your hopes for your family's future. If you're following the gist of this book, nothing in that letter should be a surprise, because you should be having those important conversations with your family all along. But this letter will reiterate those hopes and intentions and serve as a compass for your family in the midst of a difficult time.

After that, your binder needs a section on each of these areas:

- A list of key professionals or individuals to contact, like your doctor, lawyer, accountant, banker, and other advisors;

- If any of your important documents are held in a safe-deposit box, include a copy of the document with a note of the original's location;

- Copies of your medical and general powers of attorney and health care directives;

- Copies of your passport, birth certificate, and other vital records like your marriage license;

- Insurance policies like your critical illness, disability, home, and life insurance policies;

- Copies of your will and any other legal documents like trusts, marital agreements, and shareholder agreements;

- A list of your bank accounts, stock holdings, real estate, or company shares. It should clearly show what assets you hold personally, and which are held through a company or trust;

- The deed to your home and information about its purchase;

- Your investment accounts;
- Your recurring bills. An easy way to gather them together is to save all your bills and account statements for a month so that you have all of the account numbers in one place. There are even digital storage systems that can scan everything and compile it for you. You should especially make sure to keep a log of all your bills that are paid by auto-draft. Your bank account will be frozen when you die, so those auto payments will start bouncing, until an estate account is set up and appropriate banking changes made.

Your reference material should also include an inventory of your personal belongings, particularly those that have sentimental or monetary value. Go for a walk around your house with your phone and take a video of all the objects in a room. Then play it back on slow speed and see which articles you believe reflect an important family story, a memory, or a family value. Open your jewelry box or your coin collection and record the contents. Go through your valuables and ask your kids what items are special to them, or that they'd like to keep. Write down who you decide should have which items. When you're done, that video will be helpful for your homeowner's insurance, too.

> Your wealth holdings may be complicated, but your recordkeeping doesn't need to be.

The best way to create your family desk reference is to choose one member of your advisory team to help you. They can collect all the information necessary, collaborate with your other advisors, and do the detailed work of putting everything together. This reference book is your go-to so that your heirs don't need to go on a scavenger hunt or make desperate phone calls at a time when they are in an emotionally fragile state and most likely overwhelmed. It's where you put all your important information for safekeeping. It may never be complete or perfect, but don't put it off. Having it 90 percent done, or even 70 percent done, is better than having nothing done at all.

MAKE THE CONNECTIONS

Communicating your wishes to your spouse and children starts with conversations. Instead of thinking of it as a chore, think of it as a great way to spend time with your family. When we talk about money, we go deep into the bowels of who we are and what we believe. If you have the courage to think deeply about your life, your challenges and successes, you begin to unravel your "whys", your values, and your stories which truly are the fabric of your financial net worth.

The time you spend going through your personal belongings can also create special connections with your family. Whether you're talking about jewelry, paintings, furniture, or any other meaningful items, you're making a connection about family history and special memories that often transcend monetary value.

One of my clients told me about a wonderful process that his family used to share his mother's belongings after she died. They placed all the items on the dining room table and took turns, with each person stating their first choice, second choice, and so forth. As they made their choices, each person explained the reason why an item was important to them. It was slightly stressful, because sometimes people felt attached to the same items. However, by discussing *why* those items were special to them, it became much easier for the family members to let go of a second or third choice. Instead of becoming a feud, it was an opportunity to share happy memories of the mother and grandmother they all loved.

I share this idea because it's so lovely, but I still caution you not to rely on the next generation to work out their differences so amicably. These conversations can go one way or another, and there are no guarantees.

> The best way to ensure a good outcome for your estate is always to address it while you're still living.

Nobody intentionally leaves a mess for their family to clean up after them. Putting all this information together is a big project, but it's just a responsible part of life maintenance, like brushing your teeth or changing the oil in your car. You need to periodically sit down with one person and unload everything. They can put it into a nice little package for you, so your family knows what you've got and where it is.

In Chapter Nine we'll talk about the importance of keeping those documents up to date, and how to create regular habits around maintaining your financial records. Even if you update them once a year and there winds up being nine months of major changes that have to be tracked down at the time of your passing—well, that's a hassle, but it's a lot better than thirty-five years of no records at all.

✎ HOMEWORK

- Pull out your will, brush off the dust, read it and see what it states. Is everything still relevant?
- Does your will include dispositions for your personal property? Which items are special to you? Have you discussed them with your family?
- If you are a business owner living in Canada (with the exception of Quebec), do you have a business will?
- What does your family need to know in your letter of wishes? Go ahead and write it down.
- Do you have powers of attorney and healthcare directives? If you got hit by a truck and wound up in a coma, are there instructions about what you want done or not done?
- Have you executed shareholder agreements to protect your family and your business?
- Have you designated your executors, guardians, trustees, and powers of attorney? Has your relationship with them changed, so that perhaps they are no longer the "right fit"? If they are the right people to assume these roles, do they know you chose them, and why?
- Have you completed appropriate signature cards with the bank so your spouse is able to write checks, pay bills and access accounts that she may not regularly use?

> **WISE WORDS**
>
> "With a written agreement, you have a prayer; with a verbal agreement, you have nothing but air."
>
> —*Robert Ringer*

STRATEGIC ACTION PLAN

Objective:

Due Date:

Why is it important?

What will be the end result?

Who will be responsible for this project?

Who to contact:

Deadline:

Thoughts/Notes:

CHAPTER NINE

YOU'RE NEVER DONE TILL YOU'RE IN THE BOX

Review your plans regularly so you can stay current and relevant in the changes of life.

Imagine your life laid out in front of you like a photo album: your first job, your wedding, your first home together.

On the next page, your firstborn. Maybe around that time, you begin your business with great anticipation. More children. More hard work. Some ups, some downs. Maybe some very hard times.

As you flip through the pages, the years accelerate. The children grow up. Your business grows up, too. You hire more employees, purchase new buildings, add new business divisions. Your children start to bring home sweethearts, and soon you're adding new members to the family.

Here's the dream home your spouse always wanted. Here's your cottage or your vacation property at the beach. Here are your grandchildren.

With each page of this book, a new joy, a new circumstance. With each new blessing comes a new responsibility.

In your journey through life, your circumstances change, and therefore your planning must change in order to stay relevant and sustainable. The more complex your assets and your family may be, the more important it is for you to regularly refresh and reboot your planning.

I love bringing visual aids and props to client meetings, and I recently discovered my new favorite gift. Three of my clients are business partners, and I've been working with them for five years to try to get their succession and estate plans done.

Let me rephrase that—I used to have *four* clients who were business partners, and I worked with them for many years trying to get their succession and estate plans done. One of them already died, and left his affairs a little untidy, however, not too messy. The remaining three continued procrastinating. Finally, I took them all out for lunch.

"Here's my gift for you," I said. Each of them unwrapped a crystal ball.

I asked them to look into the future and tell me who would lead their business when they are gone. How would they make sure their families are taken care of, ensure family harmony and a smooth family business transition? It sounds goofy, but that little exercise helped to break through their denial and got them thinking about the future for real. It actually gave them the nudge to start getting things done with their planning.

How about you? What do you see happening in your future—children, grandchildren? A new business entity or selling one you already have? An inheritance from your own parents?

Where's your crystal ball?

If you've been following the recommendations in this book up to now, you've done a lot of work to get your plans in order. That's great! However, life doesn't stay static. Your business and your family are going to change over the next year, the next decade—the longer you live, the more change you will see. The plans that work for you today will become obsolete sooner or later. How can you stay current and relevant in the changes of life?

In earlier chapters, we talked about your intentions for your wealth. You must keep on being intentional about preparing for your future and preparing your children for their legacy. In this chapter, we'll discuss why it's so important to review and update your plans regularly, why it's so hard to stay engaged with future planning, and how you can build regular reviews and ongoing communication into your life and, most importantly, your family.

INTENTIONALITY MATTERS

You can make great decisions based on your situation today, but a lot can happen in a year that may impact those decisions. You might sell a business and incur a liquidity event. You might need new insurance, or a different type of insurance, so it makes sense to have your portfolio audited. You might decide to make a major gift to a charity or set up a loan for one or more of your children that will impact the terms of your will. Tax laws change, and you need to understand their impact on your planning goals and your hard-earned wealth. Perhaps a consideration for charitable giving might be a tax-smart way to give while you're alive instead of when you die. It makes good financial sense to dust off your plans and make sure the decisions you made last week, last month, or last year are still relevant and sustainable.

If you spent twenty-five to forty years building up your wealth for your family, it makes no sense to let hasty or outdated decisions undermine or destroy what you have built. You worked hard and long to build this legacy. Let's reflect on what you really want to happen, and the sacrifices you made—time, effort, money, relationships, perhaps even your health—in order to get here.

You need an advisor who can be a sounding board for your planning and alert you to the impact of possible changes. I've had clients sometimes call me a "consigliere," like in the *Godfather* movies. You need that consigliere who has the confidence to tell you what they know and what they don't know but can find out. They need to work with other advisors when they help you complete your annual review, and potentially be the head coach who helps you get things done.

The advisory team that we discussed in Chapter Five is important to make sure you have good advice on the different aspects of your business and estate plan. However, too many cooks spoil a broth. Your annual review should be led and handled centrally by one principal advisor who can consider your individual needs, concerns, and changes that may have occurred, gather the information from the rest of the team, and share these findings with the team, so that together they can design a single, consolidated set of recommendations that address the many moving parts of your planning.

Your advisors (or at least your consigliere) need to understand the relationships within your family, your goals, your values, your religious principles (if any), and all the different factors that go into your decision-making. They need to be willing and open to collaborate with each other and with you in preserving long-term family harmony and business continuity. And you need to be willing to invest time and money in that planning, because customized planning, clear communication with your family, and family harmony are worth far more than the wealth you have built.

KEEPING CURRENT

Keeping your plans current is like gardening. You plant seeds, and things grow. However, you have to tend your garden. You have to weed, water, and transplant. It doesn't matter whether you're growing vegetables, flowers, trees, or shrubs, you must constantly monitor, plant, prune, and mulch. You have to adapt to changing weather, pests and problems, and the health of the soil. They say the best fertilizer is the gardener's shadow.

In the same way, your own life evolves. You need to regularly review the health and relevance of your plans. Many factors can make the best-laid estate plans go stale in a millisecond: family relationships and emotions, government legislation, taxation, inflation, stock market gyrations, technology innovation, and so many more.

> **Your life circumstances evolve, so you need to regularly review the health and relevance of your estate plans.**

There are basically two options to structure a regular review of your wealth and your estate planning documents. First, you could do this review once a year, just the way you do your tax returns. You might even trigger the routine by doing it alongside your tax returns. After all, you have all the information handy at that point. The downside of pairing your review with your tax returns is that your accountant might be overwhelmed by their workload during tax season.

The other approach would be to instigate a review whenever there's a trigger event, like the purchase or sale of property or business, beginning or winding up a business venture, a marriage, the birth or adoption of a child or grandchild, or the death of a spouse or business partner. The larger and more complex your family and business enterprise are, the more trigger events you may encounter in a given year. Generally, I'd recommend the trigger-event approach for smaller or less complicated enterprises, and the annual approach for bigger families and larger businesses.

In Chapters Four and Six we discussed how your threshold of complexity changes during your lifetime. When we're younger, we have our fingers in a lot of pies and are able to juggle many different aspects of business, social life, charity, and family activities. As we grow older, we have a natural tendency to want to simplify our lives and focus deeply on the things that matter most, like family relationships, travel, exploration, or hobbies. Your business plans may need to follow that same pattern, and periodic reviews give you the opportunity to gradually scale back and simplify those plans.

Everything in business has a cost, including opportunity cost. Running a highly complex and successful family business enterprise has tremendous benefits for the economy and your overall personal wealth. A complex estate plan may have tax benefits, as well. On the other hand, they may also cost you time and money. Gradually simplifying those plans may initially cost a bit more in professional fees, but it can reduce or eliminate recurring expenses and provide more free time. The right balance all depends on your personal complexity threshold.

I'm here to tell you that oftentimes the tradeoff to simplify one's estate planning is worth it if it helps you avoid leaving a mess.

Remember your homework from Chapter Seven, where you drafted up a disaster recovery plan? The complexity of your disaster recovery plan can be a good indicator of the complexity in your overall enterprise. Make sure to review and update that plan regularly, along with your other documentation.

It is also possible that the advisors who were there to assist you as you built a successful and complex family business enterprise may not be the same advisors to help you manage your transition to a simpler structure. If your advisors don't understand that wealth can connect people and also disconnect them, they may not grasp the importance of what you're trying to accomplish. They may not have the courage to ask the more subtle questions about how you feel, current family dynamics, your fears and concerns, and how existing structures will impact your family.

If your advisors haven't suggested exploring some of the benefits of updating your plans, you may need to bring it up. Be ready to share with them your thoughts and concerns about family legacy, social capital legacy, family dynamics, business succession, taxes, and the other topics we've discussed here. Ask them if they can help you review the structures you built along the way and prune the elements that may not be serving you well anymore. It's possible that they may not know what to do or may not feel comfortable guiding you through those changes or having these softer, more personal conversations. That may be because they don't have the time and inclination. Often, it's because they are concerned about how much their time will cost you—many clients are very fee-sensitive, and they don't want to upset you with sticker shock. The reality is that a truly tailored plan based on your values, your vision, and your goals is an investment, not an expense.

Remember, though, advisory planning fees often represent a

tiny fraction of your overall wealth, if you're working with the right design team. Make sure they know you're prepared to invest what it takes. You may need to include a family enterprise advisor or other specialists to your planning team.

You should certainly ask your existing advisors for help before you venture out looking to reboot and change your team. In most cases, they should be able to give you a yea or nay, and you'll know within the first meeting—with your existing advisors or someone new—whether they are asking profound questions that will enable you to work with them on a truly customized and values-driven plan.

When you're building a new structure, you need to dig deep and see whether you hit rock, or sand, or water—or do a soil test. Likewise, a good advisor will dig deep with their questions, because they're excavating to see whether there are any cracks in your current planning foundation, or if there is a need to build a new foundation. Hopefully they will prompt you to consider things you may have never thought about.

Don't put off finding the right advisor to help you plan. A few years ago, a client referred a very close friend of his to me. I'd met the friend in passing, and he mentioned that he was interested in working with me on revising his estate plan. We got so far as to have an initial consultation where I described our process and services, how we could help him, and our proposed advisory fee. Then, nothing. For two years, he told his wife over and over that he was going to come see me soon. He was just too busy. Then one evening while watching the hockey game, he keeled back on his sofa, and boom. He was dead from a heart attack.

My client was very close to the family, so I called to offer my condolences and see how he was doing. He told me his friend's estate was a complete mess and the widow was going to call me within the next few days because she needed my help sorting everything out.

I hate to break it to you, but that's what it comes down to, really. Either you consult a professional and pay for someone to sort out your stuff now, or your loved ones will have to wade through papers, professionals, and higher fees to clean it up while they are drowning in grief. It's going to be a lot easier (and a lot cheaper) to do it now, because you can answer all the questions an advisor might have, and not leave your family guessing. Your goals and personal intentions for your family don't have to be buried with you. This is an opportunity to document your wishes while you are alive and well.

> **As the great Wayne Gretzky once said, "Procrastination is one of the most common and deadliest of diseases, and its toll on success and happiness is heavy."**

MAKE IT A HABIT

There are a number of regular habits you can (and need to) develop in order to make sure your plans and documents are up to date. We talked in Chapter Eight about legacy letters. Every time you alter your plans, leave notes (or better yet, write a letter) about your reasons for the change, and how it will impact your financial independence and your family's legacy. I can't recommend this practice strongly enough. This exercise helps you clarify your thoughts and ensures your family won't be left asking, "What were they thinking?"

I also encourage you to schedule regular family meetings. That could be as simple as a special meal around the family dinner table, or as elaborate as a group retreat. Plan to talk about philanthropy, values, family history, and your vision for the future. You might use some of the resources I recommended in Chapter Two. Include fun things to do together, and activities for all the different age groups. Preferably, hire a facilitator to help manage the "official" discussions—that way, everyone has a voice and has the opportunity to fully participate. A facilitator also helps dial down the emotional intensity and helps keep everything on track in a cordial and nonjudgmental way. A professional fee for a facilitator is nothing compared to the gargantuan cost of legal fees later if disputes arise over your estate.

I also recommend that your advisors help you prepare and regularly update a financial holdings snapshot. A snapshot is a diagram outlining all of your personal assets, your family enterprise assets, and your corporate structure, including holding companies, family trusts, and other entities. It could be a simple listing, a series of organization charts, or a full-color pictorial layout. It contains the most current information about all of your holdings and the way they relate to one another, and it should be reviewed and updated regularly.

NEVER DONE TILL YOU ARE

Once upon a time, in my early years as an advisor, I had a meeting with a client, his accountant, and his lawyer. He was incredibly successful and had recently experienced huge business growth that was set to take him to great heights. I said, "You know, if you continue along this trajectory of success, you're going to need to consider additional life insurance in order to fund the capital gains tax arising from your estate."

I don't know why, but he was very offended by this comment. In fact, he was livid. He rounded on me and said in a very terse voice, "I do not want to hear you tell me that I need more life insurance ever again, is that clear?"

Wow. I'd never seen him that angry, and later on the accountant told me he'd never seen him that angry either. Fortunately, I have the temperament and the life experience not to take it personally.

"That's okay," I replied. "But I want you to understand, with the magnitude of wealth you are building, there are taxes that must be paid when you pass away. If you don't want me to talk about insurance, I want you to sign a waiver of responsibility that absolves me if anything happens to you and leaves your affairs in a mess."

"Write it up," he snapped back. I did, and he signed it.

Don't you know, a year later he called me because he had acquired a new business along with some new business partners—and he wanted more life insurance to cover a buyout provision in the shareholder agreement. Life changed, and he came around. You don't need a crystal ball to know that your circumstances and needs are going to change and evolve with time. Review your documents regularly to make sure your planning adapts with you over time.

Life is change.

As long as you are on this earth, life keeps changing. Like the ocean, tides come in and tides go out. The sandcastle you built yesterday may be washed away and replaced by a pool full of beautiful shells. People get married, and they get married again. They have children, then more children, and then the children have children of their own. Sadly, families break apart, and then joyfully blend together in new relationships and extended families.

Businesses flourish, flounder, get bought, or sold. Property is acquired, gifted, sold, or liquidated. Legislation and tax obligations change with changing governments. The best-laid plans can become obsolete with the stroke of a bureaucratic pen.

You need someone on your team who is curious and unafraid of asking *why*, and *how*, and sometimes challenges your thought process to uncover what's really important for you and your family in the long run so they can provide appropriate solutions. And someone who has the courage to *keep* asking those questions as long as your life keeps changing. Life is change, so your planning is never done until you are done.

WISE WORDS

Never say, "That won't happen to me."
Life has a funny way of proving us wrong.

—*Unknown*

STRATEGIC ACTION PLAN

Objective:

Due Date:

Why is it important?

What will be the end result?

Who will be responsible for this project?

Who to contact:

Deadline:

Thoughts/Notes:

CONCLUSION

It was a great day for the company, but the employees didn't know it. The brand-new receptionist greeted a visitor at her desk and asked how she could help. Before he could answer, the senior security guard offered the visitor a big smile and a handshake.

"Good to see you, sir! Go right on up." The guard introduced him to the receptionist, saying, "This is the founder. He built this place!"

When the founder reached the CEO's office, he greeted one of the senior managers and paused to listen to the discussion inside. His daughter, the CEO, and his son, the CFO, were analyzing the new division they'd just launched. The founder tapped at the door and stepped in. His kids—his successors—were eager to tell him how the new plan was working out.

To be perfectly honest, he didn't completely understand the new technology they were using. It wasn't something he would have ever contemplated. Still, he clearly understood that it was a roaring success. The bootstrap business he'd grown to a hundred workers now employed more than 450. In his heyday, the company provided for his family very nicely. Now it was providing for his children's and grandchildren's households, and so many more.

Thinking back, the founder couldn't believe he'd spent so many years kicking the can on putting his long-term plans in writing. He procrastinated and complained, but he was so grateful that his advisors had challenged and pushed him to finish the project.

The family governance plan had straightened out some dicey situations with his kids' jobs, laying out clear expectations that they could all see as fair and reasonable. They had hired business coaches and other advisors to ensure that his children were well equipped with the necessary skills and guidance to become the leaders that they wanted to be. The grandchildren were benefiting from those same rules now (although somewhat modified over time), as they had the opportunity and a clear path to join the business and contribute to its success.

His own role had transitioned to semi-retirement. He enjoyed being able to come in as needed to give advice or help handle a tricky negotiation, while still having plenty of time on the golf course or traveling with his wife. He had the courage to hand the baton to the next generation, and now he was reaping the benefits.

Indeed, the time he spent with his wife was better than ever. He had great peace of mind knowing that she wasn't just provided for, she was empowered to carry on enjoying her life and the family if anything happened to him. She knew what to do and who to call for help and support. Planning their legacy together had taken their trust and partnership to a whole new level.

He was particularly grateful for his team of advisors' help in establishing the annual family retreat. What started out as an obligation where everyone felt awkward had quickly turned into a treasured tradition. Everyone looked forward to that dedicated time to enjoy each other's company, share their thoughts and hopes for the future, and learn more about the components of the family business enterprise (along with plenty of fun for the grandkids and the littlest great-grands). Those retreats were building his most important legacy, as he passed down memories and created new ones.

It was unbelievable that, through all of this, they were able to establish a family foundation that many generations would be able to participate in. He was so impressed with his kids' and even his grandkids' passion for helping others and making a positive impact in the world.

Nobody else in the building realized it, but this was a great day. They were conducting business as usual, but the stability and harmony they took for granted were actually the result of years of hard work. "Business as usual" was very, very special, and the founder was privately savoring every minute. When the CEO and the CFO finished their report, he only had one thing to say:

"Want to grab some lunch?"

Whatever your vision for your family's legacy may be, I have one compelling vision for you: that you take action. I want you to seize this opportunity to connect deeply with your family, share your heart with them, have a conversation, and follow through on providing an orderly plan for their future.

First, you must summon your courage to speak frankly about topics that are often uncomfortable, and sometimes taboo. When families can't talk about money, it hurts everyone. Then, you need to take time to understand your own story so you can share it with your loved ones. When you know where you came from and what matters to you, you can find the right path forward together.

These meaningful conversations lay the groundwork for you to prepare your family to understand and care for their legacy, so they can become good stewards. As you impart your values and train them in stewardship, you must also consider your own stewardship of everything you've built. You can direct your social capital to the causes that matter to you.

With these purposes in mind, you can choose an advisory team that asks the right questions and collaborates with each other to ensure that your financial plans embody your vision, your goals, and your values. That planning will include balancing your approach to taxes so that it is appropriate to your enterprise and your stage of life. Next, you should consider the risk factors that threaten your business, and work with your advisors to protect it. All of these plans need to be properly documented and communicated to your family, along with written confirmation of your wishes and intentions. Finally, you need to build a habit of reviewing and updating your plans regularly, so they stay current to your stage of life.

I hope you've been doing your homework all along as you read this book. Don't worry, it's not a test! Whether you did or not, there are two homework assignments I want you to complete right now, today:

First, call each of your professional advisors for a meeting, so you can ask them what role they want to play in your family legacy planning. In that meeting, ask them how they can help you protect everything you've built, prepare your heirs to manage their legacy responsibly, and ensure clarity, family harmony, and peace after you're gone.

Next, talk to your spouse. Pick a chapter of the book and ask them how you can do better at putting your plans into practice. Work together to plan a family meeting—even a meal—and consider what stories you will share.

I've mentioned several books along the way that I found helpful and formative in my own learning. I've collected those, and several others, into a list of Recommended Reading. You can find that list on my website at www.DontLeaveAMess.ca.

I can't tell you the number of times, just in an average week, that I get a call from a client, or a referred client, who says, "Oh, so-and-so needs your help. Her husband (or his parents, or their sibling) just died and left them a big mess. It's a disaster." It's such a refrain that I made it the title of my book! I don't want that to be you.

Let's make your legacy disaster-proof.

ACKNOWLEDGMENTS

The idea for this book came to me when I attended my first Strategic Coach workshop on January 27, 2000 and completing it has been a goal of mine ever since. I would be remiss if I did not acknowledge Gary Mottershead, and all the valuable team members at Strategic Coach whose insight, skill, and knowledge motivated me to actually write stuff down.

This book doesn't just distill my thirty years of experience, but also thirty years of people who have influenced me and made me a better person and a better advisor. There are so many people that have contributed to the creation of this book! My apologies, I may miss a few because sometimes I forget. My heartfelt thanks go to:

David Thibaudeau, who took a chance and hired me at the ripe young age of twenty-two to begin a career in the life insurance industry. That career evolved into intentional planning for family business owners and self-employed professionals. Dave continues to be a mentor, friend, and consigliere in my own life.

The late Gord Shipley, who also mentored me during the initial years of my career. I admire and hope to emulate his passion for helping people plan for their family's financial security, as well as his great organizational skills and personal support.

My mother, Anna Maria DeFrancesco, who modeled hard work, integrity, and humility. And my father, Bernard Pollack, who through his experience as a young widower with three young children at the age of twenty-seven, taught me the importance of being independent and finding contentment despite the difficulties of life. To my late mother, Thelma Rubin. May her memory be a blessing.

My W3 Study Group members, Terry Zavitz, Susan St. Amand, Diane McCurdy, Monette Malewski, Lynn Wintraub and Anne-Marie Girard Plouffe, all successful entrepreneurs and leaders in the financial services industry. We have enjoyed many conversations, bottles of wine, and dinners, swapping stories, sharing ideas and deepening our friendship bonds to become better at our trade for the benefit of our clients.

Todd Fithian and Robert Falvey of the Legacy Boston Group of Companies. I was searching for a like-minded group of "Legacy Thinkers," and I found you.

Lawrence Geller, a true mensch. His unwavering commitment and generosity toward helping advisors and clients understand the true value and essence of insurance, and the protection and peace of mind a piece of paper can provide, is beyond words.

Tom Deans, Ph.D., a successful author and public speaker who encouraged me to find my voice in my writing and take the risk to get it done!

The late Joe Dickstein, a legend in the insurance industry and the founder of the Broad Concept approach. May his blessed memory be a source of continued inspiration for those who were fortunate enough to know him.

James Grubman, Ph.D., whose writings inspired me to be a better advisor and begin to understand the complexities that wealth and family may create in order to help affluent families become the best they can be.

John A. Warnick, founder of the Purposeful Planning Institute. You have created an incredible organization of exceptional professionals in various disciplines who believe in constantly striving to "do good" to enable successful business families to "do great" for multiple generations. I am so thankful to have you in my world.

My valued clients who had the courage to be open to new ideas in planning when I thought there was something important and valuable to share with them.

My scribe and sounding board Ellen Seltz, my editor Nikki van Noy, my publishing manager Mikey Kershenik, and all the team at Lioncrest Publishing.

...and all the others, too numerous to mention by name, who have impacted my life and work, and encouraged me along the way. I truly work because I want to, not because I have to, and sincerely believe I have found my purpose and passion.

ABOUT THE AUTHOR

Sandy Pollack never dreamed of being a financial advisor, until her mentor (and squash coach), the late Harold Martin at McGill University persuaded her to enter the insurance industry in 1983. She got excited about helping people unravel the complexities that wealth often creates and became fascinated with the stories of her clients' lives, businesses, problems, and dreams. In 1988, she established a practice in Ottawa that became Trimaran Advisory Group LTD.

Sandy is an entrepreneurial junkie who feels strongly that entrepreneurs are an underappreciated and vital engine of any successful economy. She's passionate about disaster-proofing their complex family enterprises. She considers it a privilege and honor to serve these unsung heroes, understand their why, and help them be intentional about their legacy planning.

She's an avid reader and lifelong learner. She is a Certified Financial Planner, a Chartered Life Underwriter, a Trust and Estate Practitioner, and a Family Enterprise Advisor. She holds an MFA-P™. She is a member of Family Enterprise Canada, Purposeful Planning Institute, Conference for Advanced Life Underwriting (CALU), Society of Trust and Estate Practitioners (STEP), Family Firm Institute (FFI), and Advocis.

To request Sandy for a speaking engagement, or to order more copies of this book, email her at info@dontleaveamess.ca.

CPSIA information can be obtained
at www.ICGtesting.com
Printed in the USA
BVHW082101081122
651441BV00008B/218